CCEA GCSE
GEOGRAPHY STUDY GUIDE UNIT 2

Living in Our World

COLOURPOINT EDUCATIONAL

© 2023 Tim Manson and Colourpoint Creative Ltd

ISBN: 978 1 78073 357 9

First Edition
First Impression

Layout and design: April Sky Design
Printed by: GPS Colour Graphics Ltd, Belfast

All rights reserved. No part of this publication may be reproduced, stored in a retrieval system or transmitted in any form or by any means, electronic, mechanical, photocopying, scanning, recording or otherwise, without the prior written permission of the copyright owners and publisher of this book.

Copyright has been acknowledged to the best of our ability. If there are any inadvertent errors or omissions, we shall be happy to correct them in any future editions.

Pages 95–96 constitute an extension of this copyright page.

Colourpoint Educational
An imprint of Colourpoint Creative Ltd
Colourpoint House
Jubilee Business Park
21 Jubilee Road
Newtownards
County Down
Northern Ireland
BT23 4YH

Tel: 028 9182 0505
E-mail: sales@colourpoint.co.uk
Website: www.colourpoint.co.uk

The Author

Tim Manson learned to love Geography from an early age. He is a graduate of Queens' University, Belfast, the University of Ulster and the Open University. He has been teaching Geography for over 28 years and is the Vice Principal at Cullybackey College. He is a Principal Examiner for an awarding body in Geography and is a keen advocate for creative uses of ICT in learning and teaching. He has a highly successful website: www.thinkgeography.net

Acknowledgements

Thanks to Colourpoint for giving me the opportunity to realise a dream. Big thanks to my editor Rachel Allen, who kept me on my toes throughout, and to Wesley Johnston for the great diagrams. Thanks to Margaret McMullan for her help, advice and wise counsel through many a book and many a year. Thanks also to my colleagues at Cullybackey College who have welcomed me into the Geography fold. Thanks to my students both present and past – little did you know that you were helping to refine my ideas and material. Finally, to my wife, Helen, and to Erin and Isaac, thanks for putting up with me while I spent so much time tapping on my keyboard, and for helping make all the 'field trips' special!

Publisher's Note: This book has been written to help students preparing for the GCSE Geography specification from CCEA. While Colourpoint Educational and the author have taken every care in its production, we are not able to guarantee that the book is completely error-free. Additionally, while the book has been written to closely match the CCEA specification, it is the responsibility of each candidate to satisfy themselves that they have fully met the requirements of the CCEA specification prior to sitting an exam set by that body. For this reason, and because specifications change with time, we strongly advise every candidate to avail of a qualified teacher and to check the contents of the most recent specification for themselves prior to the exam. Colourpoint Creative Ltd therefore cannot be held responsible for any errors or omissions in this book or any consequences thereof.

This books contains URLs of websites. Colourpoint Creative Ltd has no control over the content of these sites, which could change at any time. We recommend teachers check websites prior to letting students use them. Adult supervision is essential whenever pupils access any website referenced in this book.

Contents

How to use this book 4

Study Material

Theme A Population and Migration 5
Theme B Changing Urban Areas 17
Theme C Contrasts in World Development 33
Theme D Managing Our Environment 51

Practice Questions

Getting the Best Grade Possible 66
Theme A Population and Migration 70
Theme B Changing Urban Areas 73
Theme C Contrasts in World Development 78
Theme D Managing Our Environment 82
Revision Advice 86

Glossary 89

How to use this book

This study guide is divided into two sections:

1. Study material

This addresses the key features of the CCEA GCSE Geography specification, the case studies and the key geographical terms. It also offers revision tips.

★ Key geographical terms

These key geographical terms are used throughout the specification. Each term is clearly defined.

★ Test your revision

These questions are designed to check your understanding of the course content. You can get someone to ask you the questions or test yourself.

★ Revision tip

These tips offer examiner guidance on what areas to focus on, how to avoid confusion and what might be asked in the exam.

2. Practice questions

This includes exam-style questions, tips on how to answer them and sample answers. It also offers examiner advice on how to get the best grade possible, develop your exam technique and improve your revision skills.

Study Material

Theme A: Population and migration

1. Population growth, change and structure
2. Causes and impacts of migration

Part 1: Population growth, change and structure

The 'population balance' is achieved when the number of births and deaths is equal.

> **Key geographical terms**
>
> **Crude birth rate:** The number of live births each year per thousand of the population in an area. Also known as the birth rate.
>
> **Crude death rate:** The number of deaths each year per thousand of the population in an area. Also known as the death rate.

When there is a growth in the number of people (a higher birth rate than death rate) we say that there is a **natural increase**. If there is a decline in the number of people (a lower birth rate than death rate) we say that there is a **natural decrease**.

STUDY MATERIAL

The five stages of the demographic transition model

The demographic transition model demonstrates how population changes over time. It shows how birth rate and death rate have influenced the total population of a place.

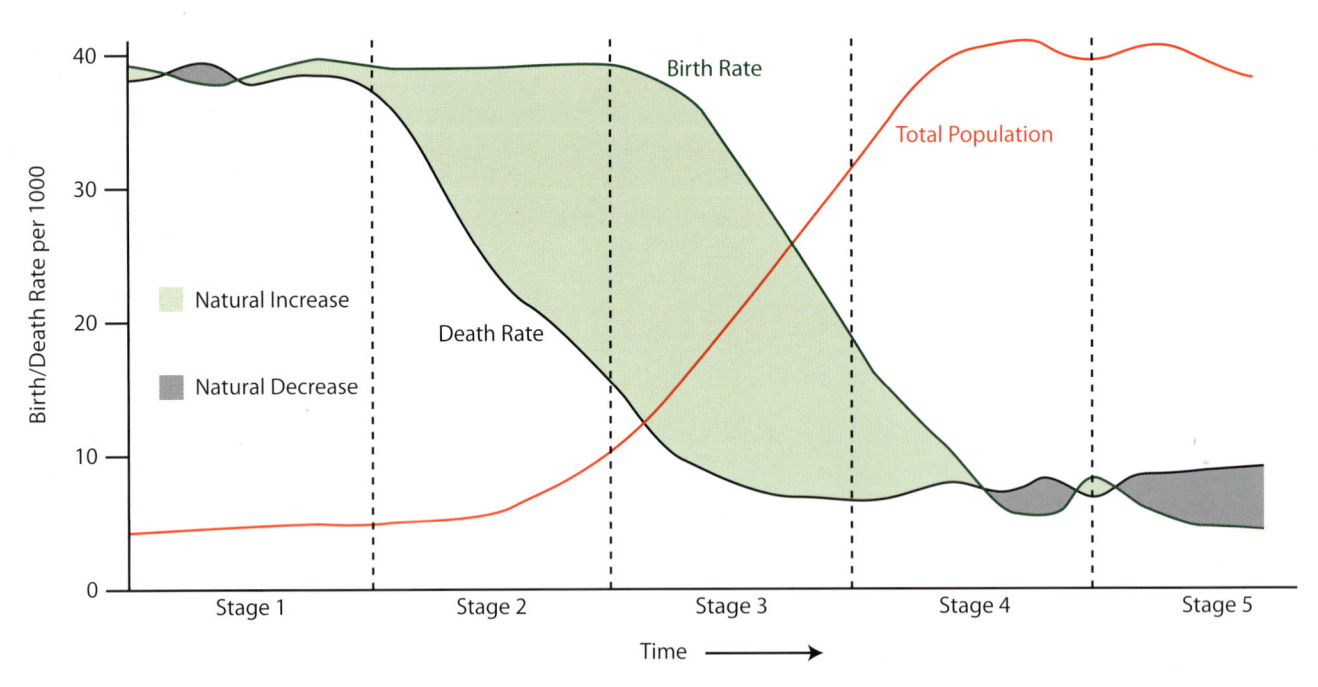

The Demographic Transition Model

The typical changes to birth and death rates in a MEDC are shown in the table opposite.

At Stage 1 both the birth and death rates are high. As time continues, the country moves into Stage 2 where the death rate drops and birth rate remains high, which causes the total population to grow quickly. The rate of increase continues to grow in Stage 3 and starts to slow down as the birth rate drops. However, the total population will continue to grow at a slower rate into Stage 4. The total population will only start to decrease during Stage 5 when the birth rate drops down below the death rate.

★ Test your revision

1. Define the term 'crude birth rate'.
2. Describe what natural increase is.
3. Explain why the death rate might decrease in an LEDC.
4. Explain some of the changes that might happen in a country to decrease the birth rate.

★ Revision tip

It is important that you can describe the birth and death rate changes in the model and explain the reasons for these changes over time.

2A: POPULATION AND MIGRATION

Stage 1 High birth and death rates	Stage 2 Death rates fall	Stage 3 Birth rates fall	Stage 4 Low birth and death rates	Stage 5 Birth rates drop below death rates
Both birth and death rates are high and fluctuate (36/37 per 1000). Many babies are being born into large families, but they are not surviving and few people are living long lives.	**Birth rates remain high but death rates fall rapidly (to 18/19 per 1000).** Life expectancy increases and death rates fall. The birth rate remains high and the difference between the two population rates is what begins the population explosion in a country.	**Birth rates fall rapidly (to around 18 per 1000) to give a slowly increasing population.** The birth rate begins to fall and social and economic pressures lead to a reduction in the number of babies born within the country.	**A form of equilibrium occurs within the population.** Both the birth rates (15 per 1000) and death rates (12 per 1000) are low and can fluctuate to give a steady population.	Some countries (mostly western European states) experience a **negative population growth** as the birth rate (7 per 1000) slips below the death rate (9 per 1000). This can produce a population that will eventually decline, as the population will not continue to replace itself.
Birth rates are high as: • There is no birth control or family planning. • Many children will die in infancy and parents will have a large number of children to ensure that some reach adulthood. • Many children are needed to work on the land. **Death rates are high due to:** • Disease, famine and poor diet. • Poor hygiene due to a lack of piped water, sewage and basic toilet facilities. • Little medical care, few doctors, hospitals or drugs.	**Death rates fall due to:** • Improved medical care, sanitation and water supplies. • Improvements in food production (both quality and quantity). • A decrease in child mortality.	**Birth rates fall due to:** • An increased use of family planning. • A lower infant mortality rate, which means that children are now surviving through to adulthood and parents do not need to have as many. • Increased industrialisation and mechanisation, which means fewer labourers are needed. • An increased desire for material possessions and a reduced interest in large families.		Population is ageing and is dominated by older people.

STUDY MATERIAL

Population structure

> ★ **Key geographical terms**
>
> **Population structure:** The breakdown of the population by age and sex in an area. It is usually presented as a population pyramid. Most geographers will refer to the young people (under 16), aged people (above 65) and the working population (between 16–65).
>
> **Population pyramid:** A graph showing the specific age and sex breakdown of a population.

Reading a population pyramid

A population pyramid helps us to see the population structure for a place. It allows us to assess the different aspects of population structure and helps us to understand the birth rate, death rate and life expectancy of people in a particular country.

Age structure of a typical MEDC

Source: Office for National Statistics. Contains public sector information licensed under the Open Government Licence v3.0.

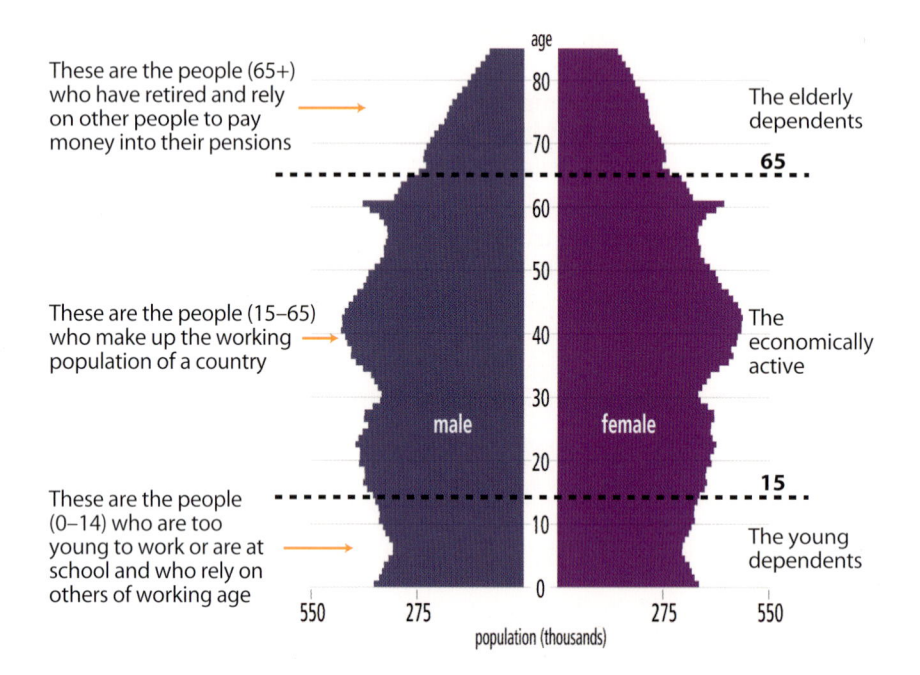

These are the people (65+) who have retired and rely on other people to pay money into their pensions

The elderly dependents

These are the people (15–65) who make up the working population of a country

The economically active

These are the people (0–14) who are too young to work or are at school and who rely on others of working age

The young dependents

Usually you will be using a population pyramid to decide whether the population is representative of a More Economically Developed Country (MEDC) or a Less Economically Developed Country (LEDC).

An MEDC population pyramid will have a much higher number of older people (at the top of the pyramid), even sides and a narrow base, whereas an LEDC pyramid will have a higher number of younger people (wide base of the pyramid), decreasing sides and a narrow top (with few people reaching old age).

2A: POPULATION AND MIGRATION

Compare and contrast the population structure of an MEDC and an LEDC

> **Key geographical terms**
>
> **Dependency:** The balance between the working population (aged 16–64) and the non-working population.
>
> **Youth dependency:** A population structure where most of the people in the population are to be found under the age of 15.
>
> **Aged dependency:** A population structure where most of the people in the population are to be found above the age of 65.

Stage	Population shape	Shape description	Key information
1 (LEDC)		Concave	High birth rate (aged under 15). High death rate (aged over 15) with a decreasing number of people in each age cohort. Very short life expectancy (around 30 years).
2 (LEDC)		Triangle	High birth rate (aged under 15). Fall in death rate (aged over 15) and slight increase in the number of people surviving in each age cohort. Still a short life expectancy (around 40 years).
3 (LEDC/ MEDC)		Tongue	Falling birth rate (aged under 15). Falling death rate (aged between 15–65). Life expectancy increases with more people living beyond 65.
4 (MEDC)		Leaf	Low birth rate (aged under 15). Low death rate (aged between 15–65). Life expectancy continues to increase with a high number of people living beyond 65. Average life expectancy reaches 75.
5 (MEDC)		Hot air balloon	Very low birth rate (aged under 15). Low death rate (aged between 15–65). Life expectancy continues to increase and average life expectancy pushes up to 85 and beyond. Population structure is very 'top heavy'.

STUDY MATERIAL

A population pyramid for an MEDC showing an aged dependent population (the UK)

Population pyramid for the UK (MEDC) in 2022
Source: Data from U.S. Census Bureau, Public Information Office (PIO)

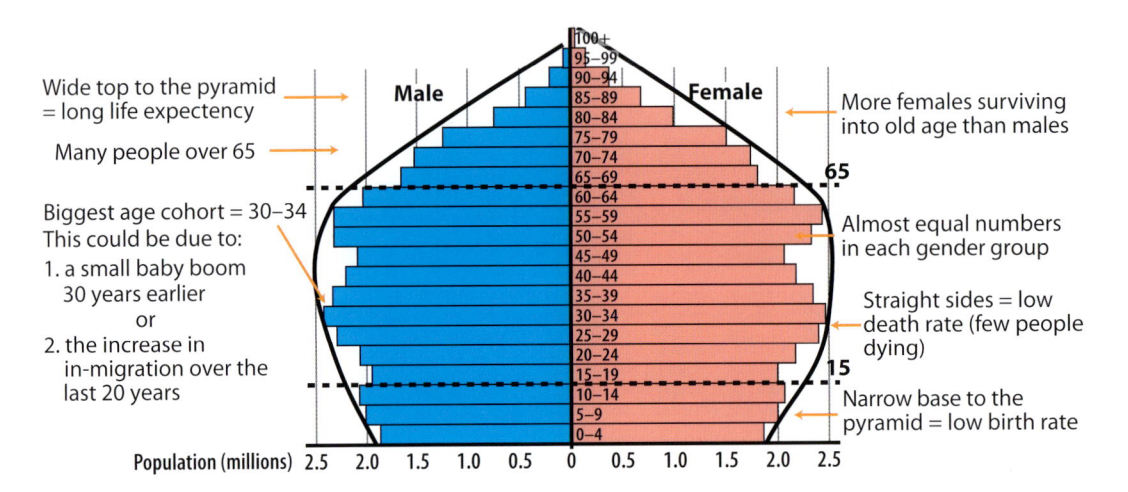

Annotations on the pyramid:
- Wide top to the pyramid = long life expectancy
- Many people over 65
- Biggest age cohort = 30–34. This could be due to:
  1. a small baby boom 30 years earlier
  or
  2. the increase in in-migration over the last 20 years
- More females surviving into old age than males
- Almost equal numbers in each gender group
- Straight sides = low death rate (few people dying)
- Narrow base to the pyramid = low birth rate

Age cohorts (y-axis): 0–4, 5–9, 10–14, 15–19, 20–24, 25–29, 30–34, 35–39, 40–44, 45–49, 50–54, 55–59, 60–64, 65–69, 70–74, 75–79, 80–84, 85–89, 90–94, 95–99, 100+

Population (millions) x-axis: 2.5, 2.0, 1.5, 1.0, 0.5, 0, 0.5, 1.0, 1.5, 2.0, 2.5

This is a population pyramid for the UK in 2022. The pyramid shape shows that the country is at Stage 4 of the Demographic Transition Model (DTM). The pyramid has steep sides as very few people are dying (death rate = 8/1,000) and the majority of children that are born (birth rate = 12/1,000) are surviving until they are 65 years old and into old age. This extended life expectancy is due to good health services. The UK could therefore be described as having an 'ageing' population. A sizeable proportion of the population is retired and older than 65 – in this case over 12.5 million people in the country. This means that the UK is increasingly becoming an aged dependency.

In MEDCs death rates have fallen due to improvements in:
- hygiene standards, sanitation, water and sewage treatment, and health education.
- medicine, resulting in cures, immunisation and vaccines.
- access to hospitals and doctors.
- diet and access to food supply.

The social and economic implications of an aged dependency

As the population continues to get older, MEDCs often experience a range of social issues that will need to be addressed by the government.

Social implications		
1. Care for the elderly:	**2. Impact on family life:**	**3. Medical issues:**
As people get older, they may need additional support at home or in residential care.	As older family members are living longer this could mean that 65-year-old children have to care for 90-year-old parents. Families might have to make difficult decisions about how to best care for elderly relatives.	With people living longer, more are suffering from 'degenerative' or long-term illnesses (such as Alzheimer's or Parkinson's disease).

2A: POPULATION AND MIGRATION

Economic implications		
1. Residential care: As people live longer, there is a greater need for support at home, accessible accommodation and residential care. These specialist services and housing can be expensive, so money needs to be put aside to pay for them.	**2. Healthcare:** Quality healthcare for elderly people can be expensive so more money will be needed to cover prescriptions, dental treatment, home visits and home help.	**3. Benefits:** Each elderly person receives a state pension. Thirty years ago the average person would claim a pension for 7 years but today this is extended to at least 17 years. This increases costs to public funds, as do other benefits, such as free public transport and winter fuel payments.

A population pyramid for an LEDC showing a youth dependent population (Kenya)

Population pyramid for Kenya (LEDC) in 2022
Source: Data from U.S. Census Bureau, Public Information Office (PIO)

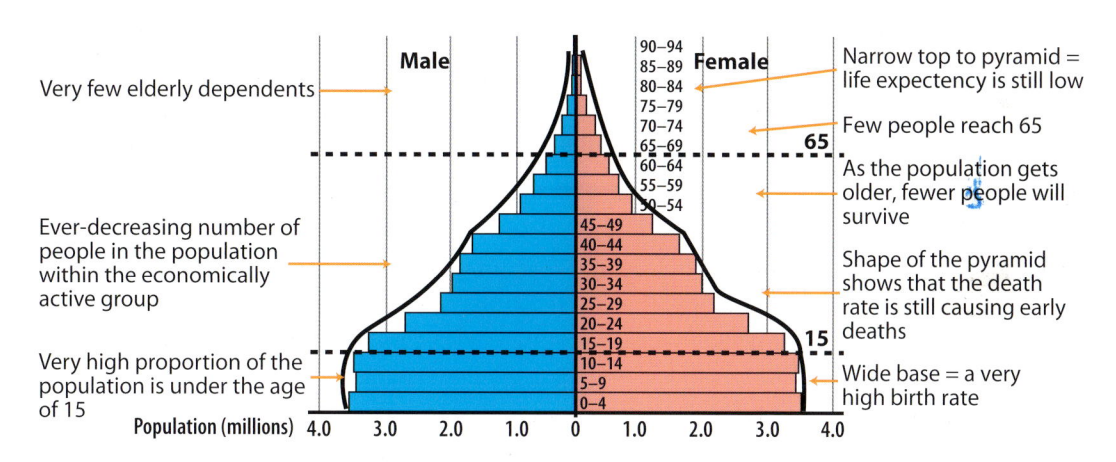

Annotations on pyramid:
- Very few elderly dependents
- Ever-decreasing number of people in the population within the economically active group
- Very high proportion of the population is under the age of 15
- Narrow top to pyramid = life expectancy is still low
- Few people reach 65
- As the population gets older, fewer people will survive
- Shape of the pyramid shows that the death rate is still causing early deaths
- Wide base = a very high birth rate

This is a population pyramid for Kenya in 2022. Over the last 20 years Kenya has remained around stage 2 of the DTM. The pyramid has a pronounced triangular pyramid shape where the number of people in each age cohort continues to get smaller. Birth rates remain high (birth rate = 20/1000) but are lower than the birth rate of 41/1000, 20 years before. Death rates have plummeted (death rate = 8/1000) but there are still few people who have reached the age of 65 or above. The wide base of the pyramid indicates the high birth rate – a high number of people within the country are aged 15 or younger. The infant mortality rate remains relatively high (about 38 for every 1000 live births).

In LEDCs birth rates are high due to the following:
- The infant mortality and child mortality rates in most LEDCs remain high. Parents tend to have larger families to ensure that some survive.
- Many people in LEDCs are subsistence farmers. They need children to provide a good supply of labour and to ensure that someone is available to care for them when they grow old.
- In LEDCs many people do not have the same access to education as MEDCs. Some people do not know how to use family planning measures and many cannot afford them.

STUDY MATERIAL

The social and economic implications of a youth dependency

As more people are born and the population increases, LEDCs often face a range of social issues due to the youthful nature of their population.

Social implications		
1. Care for young people: Many young people lose their parents to illnesses such as malaria, tuberculosis and AIDS. Their wider families, charities and churches often have to step in to take care of these children.	**2. Medical issues:** Although healthcare is improving, few doctors result in people dying from basic illnesses. People cannot afford medicine or healthcare.	**3. Opportunities/ education:** Many children in LEDCs have limited access to education, which prevents them from gaining formal skills and qualifications. This stops them getting skilled, well-paid employment and limits their opportunities.

Economic implications		
1. Education: Many LEDCs are struggling to educate the population and the limited resources for schools and universities are being stretched even further.	**2. Healthcare:** Many people cannot afford even the most basic healthcare and some die from preventable illness.	**3. Opportunities:** There is a lack of jobs and opportunities for people in LEDCs. A massive increase in the population means that there are more people now competing for the few jobs there are. Many people end up in the informal sector, often working in poor conditions for low pay.

★ Test your revision

1. Describe the shape of a population structure showing an aged dependency.
2. Describe and explain why there might be differences between the shape of the population structure in a LEDC and MEDC.
3. Explain two of the economic implications of an aged dependency.
4. Explain two of the social implications of a youth dependency.

Part 2 Causes and impacts of migration

The push and pull factors that can lead to migration

> **Key geographical terms**
>
> **Immigration:** When people move into a country. For example, migrants moving from Northern Ireland into Canada.
>
> **Emigration:** When people leave or exit a country. For example, when migrants leave Ukraine to move to Poland.
>
> **Push factors:** When a migrant is forced to leave an area. The person is motivated to move out of an area due to reasons such as war or famine.
>
> **Pull factors:** When a migrant voluntarily chooses to leave an area. The person is attracted to another area, usually looking for a better life, better standard of living or more personal freedom.

Migration: is the permanent or semi-permanent movement of people from one place to another. Migration takes place over short or long distances and it is usually a one-way movement. Some people choose to migrate (voluntary migration) while others are forced to (forced migration). Often voluntary migrants are economic migrants, choosing to move to in order to improve their standard of living, wage or job prospects. Forced migrants sometimes become refugees or asylum seekers. Migrants usually need to cross some form of administrative boundary (either at a local government or national government level) for the migration to be counted in official figures.

Key push and pull factors
People migrate for a number of reasons:

Push factors	Pull factors
• lack of services	• higher employment
• lack of safety	• more wealth
• high crime	• better services
• crop failure	• good climate
• drought	• safer, less crime
• flooding	• political stability
• poverty	• more fertile land
• war	• lower risk from natural hazards

Barriers to migration

People who are migrating may have to negotiate a number of barriers if they want to move from one country to another.

Human barriers to migration

Cost: Migration can be expensive. Money is needed for travel, accommodation and living expenses.

Legal: Migrants must have the correct documentation to move to another country, such as passports, visas and work permits. Applying for these documents takes time and is expensive. Some countries restrict the number of migrants they take.

Lifestyle: Migrating to a new place often involves a change in lifestyle, language or culture. It can be difficult for many migrants to settle down quickly.

Border protection: Many countries go to great lengths to 'protect their borders'. Border forces are often employed to carry out immigration checks and patrol along high fences and walls to try and control migrant numbers.

Physical barriers to migration

Distance: From 2012 to the present, a huge number of undocumented migrants from North Africa and the Middle East have travelled to Greece, Turkey, Italy and Spain. Although economic migrants might be able to afford to arrive by aeroplane, it can take undocumented migrants a long time to make their way across these long distances.

Deserts and mountains: There are many natural barriers that prevent migrants from moving from one place to another. Deserts and mountains can prove challenging and even dangerous to cross, particularly for illegal immigrants or refugees, who may be making the journey unprepared to escape persecution, conflict or war. Many people are intercepted and returned to their place of origin.

Seas and oceans: Throughout the recent European migration crisis, many thousands of migrants have drowned attempting to cross the Mediterranean Sea in boats that were dangerously overloaded and not fit for purpose. In 2015 alone, the Institute of Migration estimate that nearly 4000 migrants died trying to make the crossing from Africa to Europe (and a further 925,000 made it). Since 2018, there has been an increase in the number of Syrian and Iranian refugees making their way to France and attempting to cross the English Channel, in small boats, to live in England.

> **Revision tip**
>
> Make sure that you have a clear understanding of the difference between the different types of barrier that can get in the way of someone migrating from one country to another.

2A: POPULATION AND MIGRATION

The difference between an economic migrant and a refugee

Economic migrant: When a migrant chooses to move in order to improve their standard of living, wage or job prospects. Economic migrants move due to economic pressures (push factors, such as few jobs or high wages) in their origin country or economic opportunities (pull factors, such as more jobs or higher wages) in their destination country. They often want better living conditions for themselves or their families and are prepared to move long distances to achieve this. They can return to their origin country if they choose to do so.

Refugee: A person who is forced to flee from events such as civil wars or natural disasters but not necessarily facing persecution. Refugees move because they feel unsafe (push factor) in their home country. Most refugees cannot return home or are afraid to do so. Often refugees move into neighbouring countries but some will try to travel further.

Case Study: Syrian refugees arriving in Turkey (The challenges faced by both refugees and the destination country using one case study)

In 2011, the Arab Spring protests in Syria escalated into armed conflict. By 2020, an estimated 500,000 people had died due to conflict and an estimated 11 million Syrians had been forced to leave the country and become refugees. An estimated 4 million of these refugees have remained in the neighbouring country of Turkey. The Turkish government has provided more than $8 billion of aid to these refugees and has set up over 22 government-run refugee camps near the border.

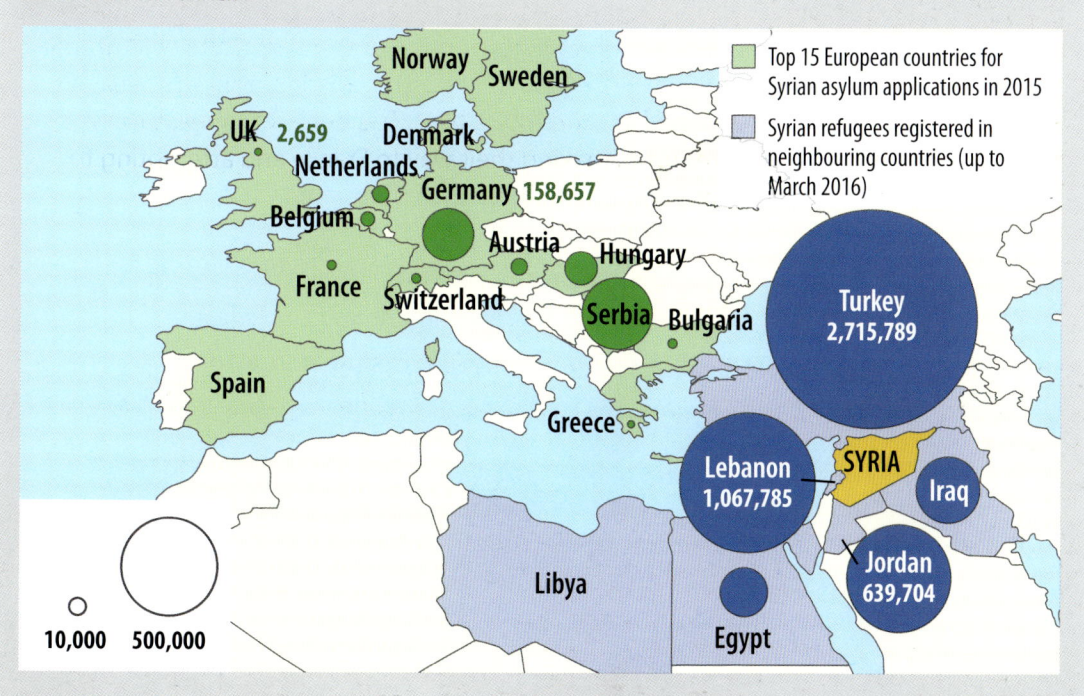

Syrian migration to neighbouring countries (in 2016)
Source: Data from UNHCR

- Top 15 European countries for Syrian asylum applications in 2015
- Syrian refugees registered in neighbouring countries (up to March 2016)

- UK 2,659
- Germany 158,657
- Turkey 2,715,789
- Lebanon 1,067,785
- Jordan 639,704

Scale: 10,000 / 500,000

15

Challenges faced by the refugees

- By 2023 there was still no solution to the Syrian conflict and refugees were frightened to return home.
- Many refugees are afraid of being classed as 'undocumented' immigrants and sent back to Syria.
- There has been conflict with the local people and anti-Syrian racism is rising in many Turkish cities. Many Syrians are now keen to move out of Turkey to avoid this conflict.
- It is difficult for refugees to find jobs and support their families. Many are working in the informal sector or the local textile industry.
- The refugee camps are temporary and lack basic facilities.
- Over 400,000 Syrian refugees continue to live in Istanbul. The competition for food and jobs can make it difficult for refugees to have good standard of living. Most end up working in informal jobs.

Challenges faced by the destination country

Over 3 million Syrians live in Turkey, putting pressure on the destination country. Recently, Turkish officials have expressed a desire for their Syrian neighbours to return home. The Turkish public have become fed up with their visitors and tired of the cultural differences and competition for jobs. For example:

- Some argue that the amount of crime in the country has increased and some Syrians have set up illegal businesses, smuggling and selling drugs.
- 74% of Syrians in Turkey would like to gain Turkish citizenship but so far only 12,000 have been approved. International organisations such as the UN and EU would like more people to be given permanent residence but the Turkish government does not want to offer this.
- The country has noticed a rise in overcrowding within its cities.
- The Turkish government is worried that the high number of refugees in the country is having a negative impact on their national security.
- Many refugees wish to seek sanctuary in Northern Europe and make their way through the west of Turkey to Greece. In 2015 alone, around 600,000 refugees are thought to have made this journey into Turkey. In August 2021, Turkey's president, Tayyip Erdoğan, said that Turkey will not become "Europe's migrant storage unit".
- Turkey has built new houses within Syria, close to Turkey's border, to host displaced Syrians. The aim is to stop more refugees coming into Turkey.

★ Test your revision

1. What is the difference between immigration and emigration?
2. Describe two push and two pull factors.
3. Explain how some migrants might experience physical barriers to their migration.
4. Describe the difference between an economic migrant and a refugee.
5. Discuss some of the challenges faced by the destination country when refugees arrive.

★ Revision tip

You may have been taught a different case study in class than the one in this book. Take care not to get mixed up between the case studies, as this will cost you marks. Make sure that you use specific facts and details in your discussion of any case study.

Theme B: Changing urban areas

1. Urban land use
2. Issues facing inner city areas in MEDCs
3. Urbanisation in MEDCs and LEDCs

Part 1: Urban land use

What is a settlement and the general function of a range of settlements?

A **settlement** is a place where people live and work. Settlements come in all shapes and sizes – they can be as large as megacities such as London (England) or Sao Paulo (Brazil), or can be as small as individual houses dispersed in a farming area such as the Lake District (England). The story behind the development and growth of each settlement is different and depends on the reasons why the particular site was chosen in the first place.

Settlement function

The **function** of a settlement relates to its economic and social activity or role, and refers to its main activities. Today, most larger settlements tend to be multifunctional (have several functions), although one or two functions might be more important than others. In some cases, the original function may no longer be applicable.

Some examples of settlement function are:
- **Market town:** Where farmers buy and sell goods and services.
- **Mining town:** Where fuel and minerals are extracted.
- **Industrial town:** Where raw materials are processed into manufactured goods.
- **Port:** A transport hub for ships on the coast, a river or lake.
- **Route centre:** Where settlement is located on junctions of several natural roads.
- **Service centre:** Where specific needs in parts of a country (e.g. farming services in an agricultural area) are provided for.
- **Cultural/religious settlement:** Where people from other parts of the world come to live and study.
- **Administrative centre:** Where government offices and general office buildings are located.
- **Residential town:** Where people live but generally work elsewhere.
- **Tourist resort:** Where people visit to enjoy themselves and their recreational needs are catered for.

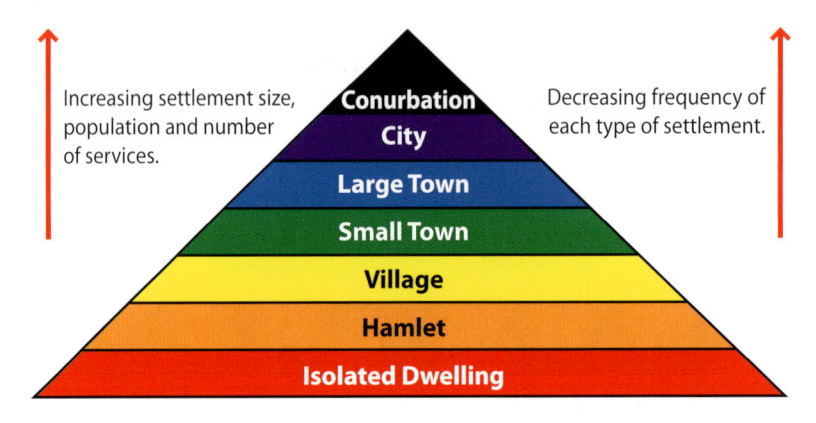

Range of settlements according to size

The characteristics and location of land-use zones

Land use can change in different sectors of the city from the central business district (CBD), through the inner city, suburbs and to the rural-urban fringe.

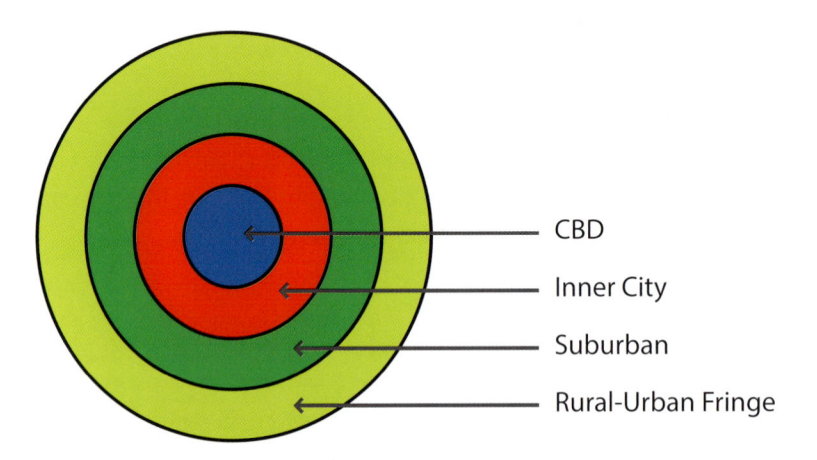

Typical shape for land-use zones in a MEDC city

> ⭐ **Key geographical terms**
>
> **Land-use zones:** A series of areas or zones within a city (CBD, inner city, suburbs and rural fringe). Land in each zone shares the same function or aspect of city life.

2B: CHANGING URBAN AREAS

Central Business District (CBD): The core of the city's business life where businesses, offices and retail are located. Peak land values occur at the centre, where there are department stores, specialist shops, public buildings, headquarters and offices for companies with large turnovers and high profits.

Inner city: The area of a city that usually surrounds the CBD. This area used to be the main source of income for the city. Here heavy industrial factories and low-cost residential areas were often built very close to each other. Houses were tightly packed into this area as people could not afford transport and needed to live within walking distance of their place of work.

Suburbs: The areas of a city that sit beyond the inner city. These areas of large-scale suburban residential development grew in the UK throughout the twentieth century. People chose to move to this space on the edge of the city to have access to larger, better-quality homes. Much of this growth was caused by an increase in car ownership and public transport, as people no longer needed to live within walking distance of their work.

Rural-urban fringe: This area of the city developed from the 1960s at the edge of the suburbs. Sometimes it can be difficult to see where the city ends and the countryside begins, as there is a mix of rural and urban land use. Urban sprawl took place with greenfield land turning into urban developments for outer-city council housing estates and private developments.

⭐ Test your revision

1. What is a settlement?
2. Define the function of a settlement.
3. Describe the difference in the functions of a market town and a port.
4. Describe the main characteristics of the central business district.
5. Explain why the inner-city areas of the city are usually found close to the CBD.
6. Explain why the rural-urban fringe has been increasing.

⭐ Revision tip

You need to understand the differences between the characteristics of each of the land-use zones in this section. Make sure that you learn the definitions carefully so that you can apply them to both short and long questions.

Basic map skills revision

> ⭐ **Revision tip**
>
> **Basic map skills**
>
> Relating to Ordnance Survey (OS) maps, the CCEA GCSE Geography specification states that students should be able to:
>
> - read maps and use the following:
>   - letter and number co-ordinates.
>   - four-figure and six-figure grid references.
>   - the eight points of the compass.
> - identify features on a plan or map by using symbols and a key.
> - demonstrate knowledge and understanding of scale by measuring area, straight line distances and curved line distances.
> - demonstrate knowledge and understanding of how relief is represented on OS maps (1:50,000).
> - identify major relief features.
> - relate cross-sectional drawings to relief features.
> - analyse the interrelationship between physical and human factors on maps.
>
> (Source: © CCEA 2023: Reproduced with permission of the Northern Ireland Council for the Curriculum, Examinations and Assessment.)

Scale and distances

Scale takes real life things and reduces them in size many times so that they can be shown on a map. The Ordnance Survey (OS) maps used in the exams will be at a scale of 1:50,000. This means that 1cm represents 50,000cm (500m / half a kilometre) or 2cm = 1km.

- ***Measuring a straight line distance***
  The easiest way to work out distance is to use a ruler to measure from one point to another on the map and then use the scale to work out the distance in kilometres. In the example opposite, the distance has been measured as 6cm, which is equivalent to 3km of real distance.

- ***Measuring a route (non-straight line) distance***
  In an exam, the best way to measure a route or non-straight line distance is to use the edge of a piece of scrap paper.
  1. Place the corner and straight edge on your starting point.
  2. Pivot the paper until the edge follows the route you want to take.
  3. Every time the route changes direction, make a small mark on the edge of the paper and pivot it so that the paper follows the route again.
  4. Repeat this process until you complete your route.
  5. Measure the distance from your first mark to your last mark on the paper. Then use the scale to work out the distance in kilometres.

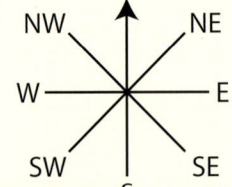

Eight points of the compass

There are eight points on the compass. You can use these to state the direction of one feature or place from another.

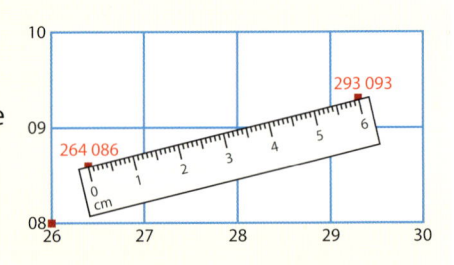

2B: CHANGING URBAN AREAS

Grid references
OS maps are covered in a series of blue grid lines. These grid lines help you to pinpoint an exact location on the map through the use of a unique number called a grid reference.

- **Four-figure grid references**
  A four-figure grid reference will help you to identify the location of a square on the map. Read the number along the bottom or top ('along the corridor'), followed by the number up the side ('up the stairs'). In the example opposite, all of the symbols are found in square 1321.

- **Six-figure grid references**
  A six-figure grid reference will help you to identify the precise location of a point *within* a square on the map. The first two numbers ('along the corridor') and the fourth and fifth numbers ('up the stairs') indicate the square that the point is found within. The third and sixth numbers are gained by drawing an imaginary grid on top of the square and assigning a number from 0 to 9 across the square.

In the example opposite, all of the symbols have a four-figure grid reference of 1321 but only one symbol has the precise location of 132212. Which one? It might help to actually draw the grid (until you get the hang of it) but you will not have time to do this during an exam, so you have to practise this skill. What are the precise six-figure grid references for the other symbols in this square?

Using symbols
Symbols are used on maps to represent important features, so that the map does not become too cluttered. The good news is that any map you get in an exam will have a key attached, so you do not need to learn the symbols. However, it is a good idea when revising 'Changing urban areas' that you are able to identify some of the main features found in urban areas. Sometimes, it is harder to pick out map symbols in urban areas than in more remote rural settings.

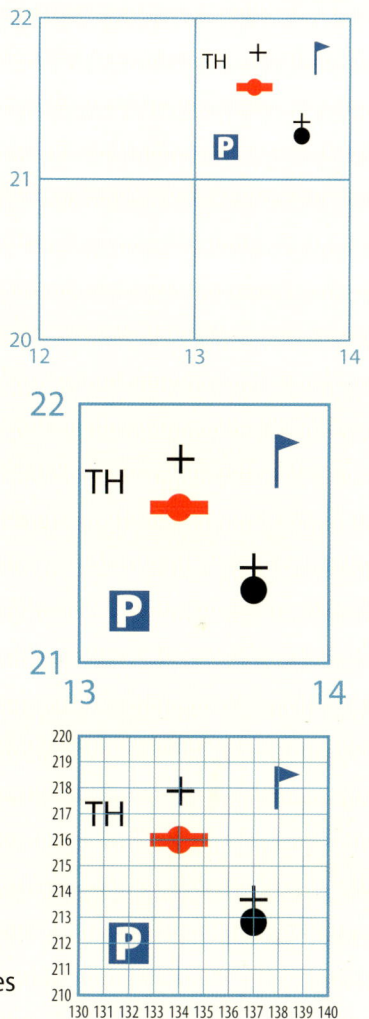

General features

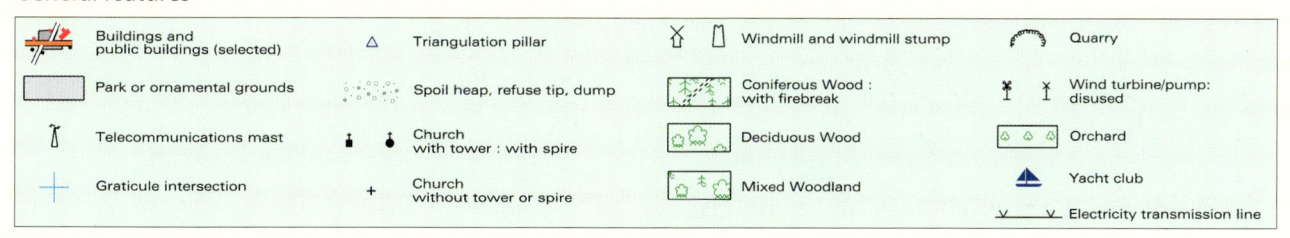

Symbol	Feature	Symbol	Feature	Symbol	Feature
	Buildings and public buildings (selected)	△	Triangulation pillar		Windmill and windmill stump		Quarry
	Park or ornamental grounds		Spoil heap, refuse tip, dump		Coniferous Wood: with firebreak		Wind turbine/pump: disused
	Telecommunications mast		Church with tower : with spire		Deciduous Wood		Orchard
	Graticule intersection	+	Church without tower or spire		Mixed Woodland		Yacht club
							Electricity transmission line

Tourist information

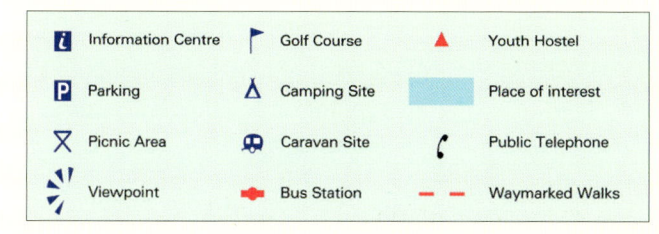

Symbol	Feature	Symbol	Feature	Symbol	Feature
i	Information Centre		Golf Course	▲	Youth Hostel
P	Parking		Camping Site		Place of interest
X	Picnic Area		Caravan Site		Public Telephone
	Viewpoint		Bus Station	--	Waymarked Walks

This is based upon Crown Copyright and is reproduced with the permission of Land & Property Services under delegated authority from the Controller of Her Majesty's Stationery Office, Crown copyright and database right 2023 PMLPA No 100496

STUDY MATERIAL

Interpret aerial photographs and maps to identify:
- **the general functions of a range of settlements; and**
- **the land use zones of the settlements**

Aerial photos (and maps) can be used in exam papers. Students need to be able to find and identify information that suggests a particular function or land-use zone in a settlement.

Aerial view of Belfast
Image captured by Colin Williams Photography

The aerial photo above shows some of the different land-use zones in the city of Belfast. It is important to look for characteristics typical of the land use in each part of the city.

Land use zone	Description	Observed Characteristic
Zone A	Central business district (CBD)	Tall buildings and office blocks at city centre.
Zone B	Inner city	Area of compact rows of terraced housing close to industry.
Zone C	Suburbs	Larger houses with gardens and garages that are farther away from the city centre.
Zone D	Rural-urban fringe	Houses built on the edge of the city.

2B: CHANGING URBAN AREAS

Part 2 — Issues facing inner-city areas in MEDCs

MEDC inner-city areas grew quickly in response to the Industrial Revolution from 1815 onwards. The rate of growth was controlled by how much industrialisation was taking place in the city and how many factories were being set up for heavy manufacturing.

Housing

The rapid growth of the MEDC inner-city often meant that cheap, poorly-constructed houses were built close to factories. The houses were small and often overcrowded, with two rooms (a living room and pantry) downstairs and two bedrooms upstairs. In the early 1900s, the average household size was eight people (two adults and at least six children) and all these people had to be squeezed into two small bedrooms. Outside toilets were the norm and from 1900 there might have been one tap to provide clean drinking water downstairs.

Poor-quality housing

Following the Second World War, many of the houses were over 100 years old. The inner-city areas started to become increasingly out of date and lacked basic facilities and room for modern appliances. In the 1960s, many people started to move to larger, more modern houses in the suburbs, which caused a further decline in the inner-city areas.

In the 1960s and 1970s, houses in the inner city were in poor condition and much of the heavy industry was in decline. The factories had closed and manual work was increasingly scarce. People had to travel to the edge of the city or move to other places for work. Those who were left had less money to spend, and shops and services began to close down.

Eventually the government decided to modernise some of the inner-city housing. Families could apply for improvement grants to help make basic improvements to their houses.

Old derelict houses in Battenburg Street, West Belfast, in 2015, that have now been redeveloped

Gentrification

Urban regeneration is when an urban area is upgraded. The aim is to improve both the economic and social spaces within a city. It usually happens to areas where there is dereliction, pollution or out migration. It might allow some buildings to be restored (with old buildings being repurposed for a different use).

Gentrification is when richer people move into an urban area and replace the poorer people who used to live there. This changes the character of an area. The area is redeveloped and upgraded, attracting more rich people and raising property prices. This means that the original residents are never able to afford to move back into the area.

Main features of gentrification

Positive features	Negative features
• Old, dilapidated houses are improved and modernised.	• A high demand for houses can increase competition and push prices up.
• House prices increase over time.	• Higher house prices force original residents out of the area.
• New business opportunities come in to provide services to the new community.	• There might be some conflict between the original and the new residents.
• Crime rates decrease.	

In Belfast, one such gentrification programme began in the late 1980s. The Laganside Corporation was set up on the banks of the River Lagan in central Belfast to develop a 300-acre stretch of land to the east of the CBD that had been experiencing high levels of deprivation and unemployment. Some old, terraced houses were removed and new apartment blocks with views over the River Lagan were built. However, the cost to rent or buy these apartments was too expensive for the people who had originally lived there and they were displaced to other parts of the city.

Traffic

Most MEDC inner-cities were built so that people lived close to their place of work. This meant workers could walk to work. However, since the 1950s, the amount of traffic on the roads has increased at a massive rate and in the 1970s car ownership began to grow. According to the most recent census, most people living in Belfast city have access to their own car and this has been putting pressure on the roads and traffic infrastructure. In Belfast City Council, 122,000 cars or vans are available for a population of 144,000 people.

Roads expert Wesley Johnston noted that:

> "This is in keeping with all UK cities, but the effect is more pronounced in Belfast due to The Troubles … as buses were routinely being hijacked, and encouraged a greater degree of movement to the suburbs."

Source: 'Belfast UK's most congested city with drivers stuck in jams 200 hours a year', *Belfast Telegraph*, 21 February 2017

Congestion (air quality and journey time)

Congestion has become a major issue for many MEDC cities. A report in 2017 noted that Belfast was the UK's worst city for traffic congestion, with drivers likely to spend over 200 hours a year stuck in traffic jams (an average of 8.3 days a year). Belfast has tried a number of measures to reduce congestion in the city. The Westlink was completed in 1983 to link the two main motorways that flowed into Belfast. The M3 Lagan Bridge opened in 1995. These two projects helped to reduce congestion for a time but journey times started increasing again as more and more people used their own private transport. Some blamed the lack of adequate public transport.

In January 2019, the government published a clear air strategy aimed at reducing the amount of road traffic emissions across Northern Ireland. Its report noted than nitrogen oxide pollution from traffic was a 'significant problem' and people were not switching to use public transport.

In London, Transport for London introduced a congestion charge in 2003 to try to limit the number of people who were driving into the city centre. As a result, nitrous oxide levels fell by 13.4% between 2003 and 2007, particulates fell by 24%, and carbon dioxide levels by 3%. Currently the congestion charge is £15 but a new Ultra Low Emission Zone was also introduced in 2019 to help improve air quality in the city. This charges most vehicles a further £12.50 a day.

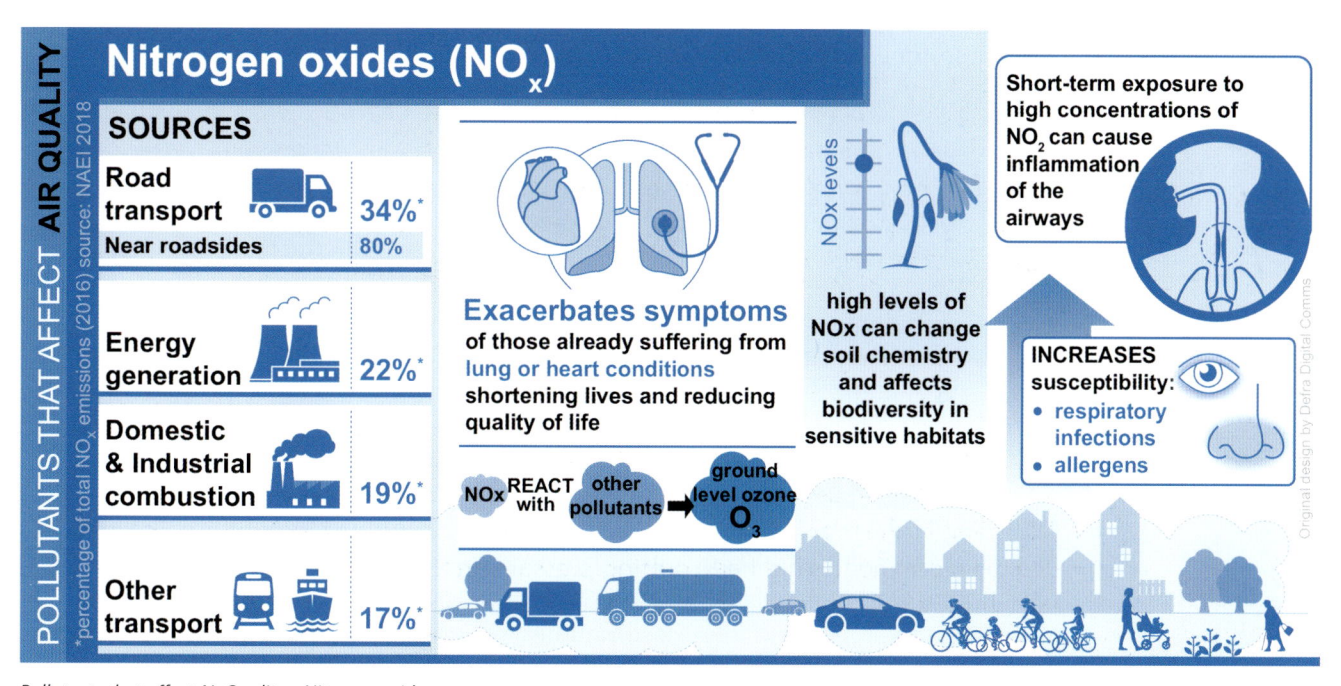

Pollutants that affect Air Quality – Nitrogen oxides
Source: 'Clean Air Strategy 2019', Department for Food Environment & Rural Affairs, © Crown copyright 2019. Contains public sector information licensed under the Open Government Licence v3.0.

Public transport (cost and efficiency)

The UK government has invested a lot of money into the public transport network (such as train, underground and bus services) to encourage commuters to use public transport rather than cars. In many cases the transport links are integrated together to allow people a smooth transition from one transport type to another.

In reality, many people find it difficult to use public transport. Using public transport can be very expensive, e.g. a weekly train ticket from Mossley West (Newtownabbey) to Central Belfast costs around £25 per week, £100 per month, £1200 per year. Another issue is that car parking can be difficult at the station, as there are not enough spaces for all of the commuters. Also the trains run only every hour and each train is very overcrowded as the capacity has been reached. Further investment is needed to put trains on more frequently.

Parking (cost and availability)

The cost of parking in the CBD and inner cities has risen rapidly over the last few years. In part, this is to discourage driving into the city and to encourage public transport use. However, it is also to collect as much money from people as possible. High parking costs combined with expensive and inaccessible public transport has been blamed for the decline of many city high streets. Many on-street and high-rise parking facilities are available in the city (at a premium price). However, at peaks times (like Christmas) it can be difficult to find a parking space, which can cause further congestion in the city. In Belfast, there has been conflict between local residents (e.g. in the Markets area) and commuters who both try to park their cars on inner-city streets.

Any strategy to remove parking from city centres (with an increased focus on public transport) needs to include adequate and appropriate spending on public transport to ensure that people can actually get into the city. Public transport also needs to be affordable, for example, often it is more cost efficient for a family to pay parking for one car in the city centre, rather than multiple individual public transport fares.

Cultural mix

Cities are places where migrants find sanctuary. They are often the first place that immigrants go to find people from similar backgrounds who might help them get established in their new country. As a result, the inner-city areas, with their cheap housing, often become places where there is a large transient population and an ever-increasing ethnic diversity.

Ethnic tensions

Migrants bring a lot of positives to the inner city – they bring new cultures, religions, race, languages, dress, food and music. However, when people from a different ethnic background start to move into an area, tensions may develop. The original residents might feel threatened and this can sometimes lead to conflict and violence. For example, MEDC cities such as New York, Manchester and London can experience conflict and ethnic violence when groups of people with different ethnic backgrounds live near each other.

In Belfast, the population of people who come from different ethnic backgrounds is on the increase. Nearly 10% of residents were born outside of Northern Ireland. Concentrations of people from China, Syria, Romania, Poland and Turkey can be found in some inner-city areas in the east and south of the city.

London has a population of 8.6 million with roughly around 44% of the population identifying as black or from a different ethnic minority.

Religious tensions

Migrants will continue their different religious practices as they move into new cities. The UK has operated a 'multiculturalism' policy for many years, which means that it allows people to practice their own religion. In her 2019 Easter message, the UK Prime Minister noted that the people of the UK share "values of compassion, community and citizenship" where people could enjoy religious freedom. However, some people are intolerant of religious beliefs different to their own. This can lead to discrimination and violence.

In Belfast, tension between some sections of the Catholic and Protestant communities led to a conflict called the Troubles, which cost the lives of over 3500 people. Even today, tensions occur over marching, flags and commemorating the past.

Language barriers

With increased immigration, the number of people who do not speak English or who speak English as a second language in UK cities is increasing. This can make it difficult for migrants to communicate and access services. It also puts pressure on government services in health and education to provide leaflets and translation services across a range of languages.

Test your revision

1. Describe two housing issues in the inner city.
2. What part does gentrification play in changing cities?
3. Describe how traffic congestion is an issue in MEDC cities.
4. Describe how public transport and parking are issues for the inner city.
5. Explain how ethnic tension can influence the cultural mix in a city.

Revision tip

You need to understand the issues that help to create problems in the inner-city areas within MEDC cities. Try to include examples from cities that you know, such as Belfast.

Part 3: Urbanisation in MEDCs and LEDCs

Urbanisation is an increase in the proportion of people living in towns and cities, which usually takes place as a result of rural-urban migration.

An **urban planning scheme** is a plan put into place (usually by the local government) to change and improve the urban environment. Planning allows any changes to occur in an organised, methodical manner that will add value to an area.

Case Study: Inner-city Belfast (an MEDC city)
(an urban planning scheme that aims to regenerate and improve the inner city)

Belfast is a good example of a city that has had to deal with issues in poor, old areas of the inner city. Over time a number of strategies have been used to re-develop parts of the city and in particular the Belfast Harbour area. All of these have fallen under the Belfast Metropolitan Area Plan (BMAP).

- The Laganside development began in 1989 with the building of the Lagan Weir (at a cost of £14 million), which controlled the amount of water in the river and kept the mudflats covered at all times.
- Much of Belfast's traditional manufacturing had grown up in Queen's Island but the decline of Harland and Wolff from over 20,000 workers to 500 in 2002 meant that there was around 185 acres of land that was not being used to its full potential.
- There was a need for further development in this industrial area of Belfast and in 2006, the Titanic Quarter development planned to reinvent this brownfield site into a new, fresh, modern space where people would come to live, work and play.

Titanic Quarter, Belfast
Improvements that the Titanic Quarter brought to Belfast

Housing
- The proposed 5,000 dwellings in Titanic Quarter should provide residential accommodation for around 20,000 people.
- By 2009 only 474 dwellings were completed (in the Arc complex).
- In 2022, Belfast City Council announced that it had given permission for an additional 778 dwellings to be built by 2025. This is to include build to rent, social and affordable housing. A park and public walkway are to be included in the plans.

Transport
- The BMAP (Belfast Metropolitan Area Plan) planned to improve transport links in the area, especially in relation to the public transport networks.
- New bus services, walkways, bridges and cycle routes were developed in order to reduce congestion and air pollution across the city. This included the new Glider buses which run through the Titanic Quarter and link it across the city of Belfast.

Image captured by Colin Williams Photography

Employment
- The £7 billion development was expected to create 25,000 jobs over the next 15 years. Initially these were in construction but now include IT and financial services (Microsoft, Google, NI Science Park and Citibank/Citigroup), hotels (Premier Inn and Titanic Hotel), visitor attractions, car show rooms (Audi/Porsche) and the film industry (in the old Harland and Wolff Paint Hall).
- The types of job that the Titanic Quarter is bringing to the city are very different to the old heavy manufacturing that used to be on the same site. These jobs require new skills, new qualifications and new employees, which should help improve the diversity of the city.

Environment
- In the building of the Titanic Quarter, any industrial pollutants had to be removed from the site.
- A process of soil remediation was carried out where land contaminated by the shipbuilding industry was restored.
- Visually, the area has also been much improved.

Evaluation of this urban planning scheme

Titanic Quarter continues to grow. The Titanic Hotel opened in 2017, 'We are Vertigo' continues to expand and new jobs have been created with the opening of the Amazon distribution centre.

Housing	• Nearly 500 apartments have been built as part of the Arc complex near the Odyssey. However, the 2009 economic recession had a major impact on this area and residential building slowed until 2022. • Some local residents have complained that many of the shops, restaurants, transport and services that they were told would be provided have not materialised. • The BMAP incorporates both social and gentrified housing schemes, allowing people with various incomes to live in the areas close to their employment. • The apartments built in Titanic Quarter provide more housing units than individual houses, giving the development a smaller 'urban footprint'. This reduces heating bills and allows services such as water supply and bin collections to be shared. • Modern construction is designed to provide a light and attractive environment. People are encouraged to take pride in their areas, developing a sense of community and safety in the urban landscape.
Employment	• The number of jobs in Titanic Quarter continues to rise. However, these are usually given to people who do not live in the immediate area. The ideal of people living and working in close proximity has not happened. • There is a broad range of jobs from people in the service and tourism industries, retail, financial services, IT, the TV and Film industry, and education (QUB and Belfast MET have campus facilities in the area).
Environment	• There is no doubt that the area is environmentally better than it was in its industrial past. • Major efforts have been made to ensure that the area is clean, free from pollution and looks after local animal life. • The regeneration of the Belfast Harbour area removes much of the old water and pollution of its industrial past. • The developers of Titanic Quarter are committed to the reduction of waste and the recycling of waste materials. • It is more sustainable to reuse this land than to develop greenfield sites at the edge of the city. • Although there are urban walkways, there are no real parks or natural areas with planted trees.
Transport	• Initially, the transport plans for the area included the development of a tram system that would connect into wider Belfast. • This was replaced with the more cost-effective Glider system. These are diesel-hybrid articulated buses. They are better for the environment but are not totally carbon free in their output. They provide a more environmentally-friendly transport route for those coming to work in this part of the city. • The transport into the area is cheap, regular and easy to use. • Some have argued that the service to this part of the city is still too sporadic and needs further investment.

STUDY MATERIAL

⭐ Test your revision

1. What does the term 'urban planning scheme' mean?
2. Describe some of the ways that Belfast has attempted to regenerate in recent years.
3. Evaluate an urban planning scheme that you have studied with reference to housing and transport.

⭐ Key geographical terms

Shanty town: A spontaneous settlement built within a city. Also known as a favela. This area often features unplanned, poor-quality housing and lacks basic amenities, such as clean water.

Case Study: Sao Paulo (an LEDC city)

(The location, rapid growth and characteristics of shanty town areas in an LEDC city)

Location:	South-east Brazil, 30 miles from the Atlantic Ocean.
Population:	An estimated 20 million people in the wider metropolitan area.

The location and growth of Sao Paulo

Many LEDC cities have grown due to the push and pull factors that operate in an area. The favela regions of the city have grown either on the edge of the CBD in old inner-city brownfield sites or at the edge of the city. In either case, the land is usually very poor, part of a rubbish dump or on land that is considered to be too steep for normal building practices.

The location of Sao Paulo

Push and pull factors

Rural 'push' factors

Many people feel forced out of the countryside because:

- mechanisation means that there is less need for labour on farms.
- people are starving, either due to too little output from farms or crop failure and drought.
- there are few employment opportunities.
- there is overpopulation, resulting in high birth rates.
- there is pressure on the land (due to subdivision in families).

30

2B: CHANGING URBAN AREAS

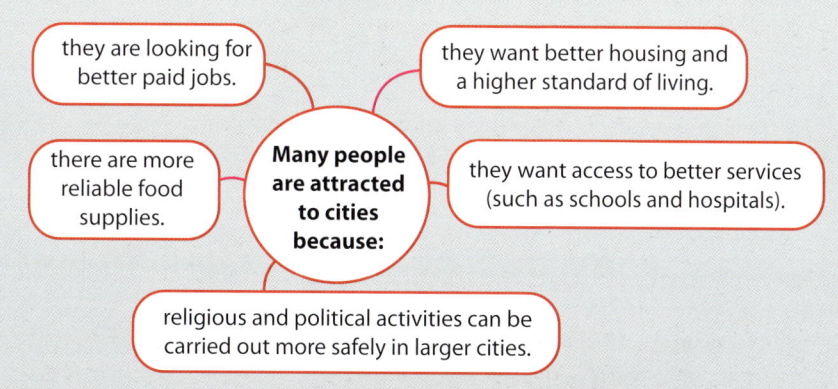

Urban 'pull' factors

Many people are attracted to cities because:
- they are looking for better paid jobs.
- they want better housing and a higher standard of living.
- there are more reliable food supplies.
- they want access to better services (such as schools and hospitals).
- religious and political activities can be carried out more safely in larger cities.

Causes of urbanisation

A rapid increase in population	Pull factors that brought people to Sao Paulo	Push factors that moved people out of rural areas
Large numbers of migrants moving from the poor, agricultural north-east regions of Brazil to Sao Paulo.	Good employment opportunities, with 50% of all Brazilian industry in Sao Paulo (construction, manufacturing and mining).	Farming was poorly paid and hard work. The perception was that work in the city was easier and better.
A lot of international migration as many people from Portugal, Italy and Germany made their way to Sao Paulo.	Good transport links (roads and railways) made it easier to migrate.	Rural areas have poor services compared to the big city.
High natural increase due to high birth rates and a lowering of the death rate.	Good access to services such as schools and hospitals can encourage people to move into the city.	Famines and drought put a strain on life in rural areas.

Characteristics of the Sao Paulo shanty town (favelas)

A favela is a 'spontaneous' settlement. The local councils in Sao Paulo define it as being "an illegal occupation of terrain in a city where dwellers often have to live without basic infrastructure, such as water, sewage, electricity, garbage collection, mail, etc."

Location
- As migrants arrive in Sao Paulo, many move to the informal favela settlements and build makeshift homes, constructed out of whatever materials they can find.
- The favelas are mostly built on wasteland, marshy land, land that is likely to flood or very steep slopes, where no other building would be possible. They are usually near transport links, rivers and rubbish dumps.
- Many of the bigger favelas in Sao Paulo are located on the outskirts of the city. The biggest is called Heliopolis and is found in the south-west area of the city. It has an official population of 200,000 people but the true population is probably much higher than this. The second biggest, Paraisopolis (Paradise city) is located farther away to the south and has a population of around 100,000 people.

Growth
- The rapid increase of the population of Sao Paulo is estimated at 2000 new migrants arriving into the city each week.
- Favelas grew at a fast rate, by an estimated 120.6% at their peak from 1980–1990 and 57.9% from 1991–2000.

Key characteristics of the shanty town (favela)

Transport and traffic
There is a high dependence on the public transport system and it is struggling to cope. Congestion and traffic jams are common and there is much noise and air pollution.

Services
Basic services are limited in the favelas, with access to electricity, clean water, schools or doctors sporadic. Sewage often contaminates the water supply leading to health issues and disease, such as typhoid and dysentery.

Pollution
An industrial haze, intensified by traffic fumes, often hangs over the city. The city produces large amounts of waste which, in the favelas, is unlikely to be collected. Its presence, combined with polluted water supplies and sewage in open drains, can cause further health hazards.

Employment
There are not enough jobs and people are forced to work in the informal sector, where they provide basic services for a small fee, e.g. roadside fruit selling, cutting hair, shoe shining and collecting rubbish.

Crime
The favelas are perceived as containing a lot of organised crime, violence and drug-trafficking.

Housing
Poor residents live in permanent but poor-quality housing between the inner city and the suburban favela, or in the very poor-quality conditions of the shanty towns. One third of the population of Sao Paulo is estimated to live in one-roomed dwellings.

Segregation
There is a very big divide between the rich and poor, and little social interaction between the different groups.

★ Test your revision

1. Describe two push factors that might encourage people to move into the city.
2. Describe two pull factors that have encouraged the growth of the shanty town.
3. Describe the location of the shanty town (favela) in Sao Paulo.
4. Describe and explain some of the characteristics of the Sao Paulo shanty town.

Theme C: Contrasts in World Development

1. The development gap
2. Sustainable solutions to deal with the problems of unequal development
3. Globalisation

Part 1: The development gap

Identify the differences in development between MEDCs and LEDCs using social and economic indicators

> ⭐ **Key geographical terms**
>
> **Development:** The quality of life of humans within a country or area. It is linked to the wealth and progress of the area.
>
> **The development gap:** The difference in economic activity, wealth and social measures between the rich MEDCs and poorer LEDCs.
>
> **MEDC (More Economically Developed Country):** Usually a rich country found in Western Europe or North America.
>
> **LEDC (Less Economically Developed Country):** Usually a poorer country found in South America, Africa or Asia.

Development is linked to the economic wealth or progress that is experienced within a country and considers how foreign aid, political decisions, healthcare, education, poverty, infrastructure, human rights and the environment all work together to determine the quality of life.

There is often a large and widening difference between the quality of life experienced by a person living in an MEDC compared with that of someone living in an LEDC.

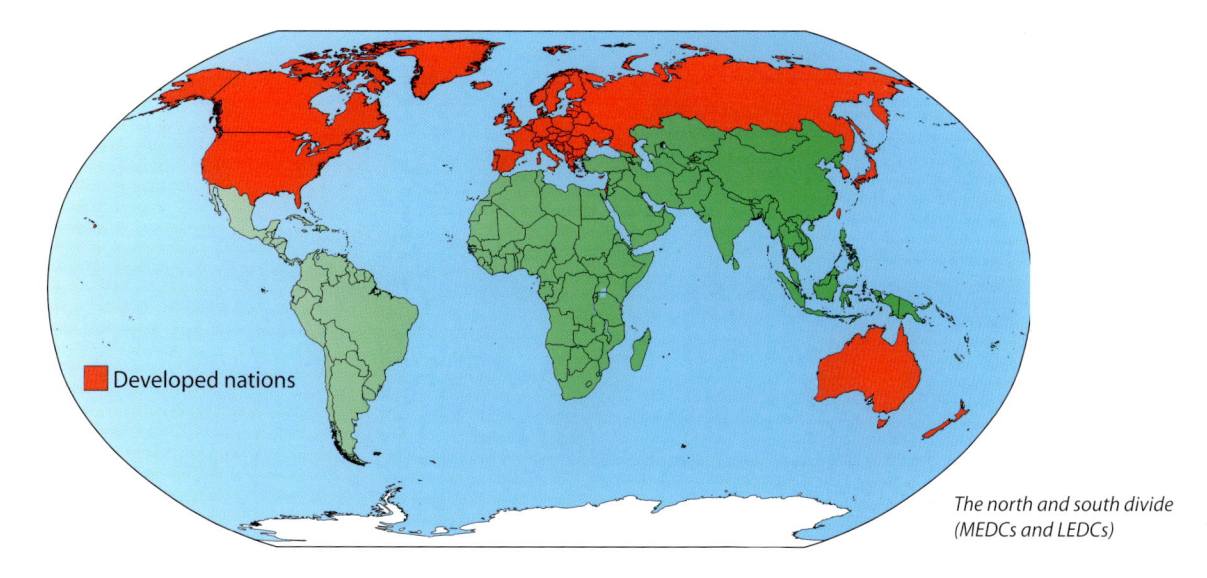

The north and south divide (MEDCs and LEDCs)

STUDY MATERIAL

The indicators used to measure development

Key geographical terms

Social indicators: A set of factors used to assess how well a country is developing in the key areas that affect people, such as health, education and diet.

Economic indicators: A set of factors used to assess the amount of money or wealth within a country and how the people actually earn that wealth (e.g. GNP or GNI).

Social indicators

1. Health
- *Life expectancy* shows the average lifespan of someone born in that country. The higher the life expectancy, the more developed the country is (e.g. UK = 80 years and Chad = 52 years).
- *The number of patients per doctor* shows the inequality in healthcare provision between north and south. People in LEDCs have less access to doctors (e.g. Zambia = 1 doctor per 12,00 patients) than people in MEDCs (e.g. UK = 1 doctor per 314 patients).

2. Education
- *Adult literacy rate* has been used for many years to show the percentage of the adult population who are able to both read and write. In the UK and other MEDCs you would expect this to be 99%, however, in Somalia (an LEDC) only 40% of adults can read and write.

Economic indicators

1. Gross National Income or Gross National Product (per capita)*

GNI shows the total economic value of all of the goods and services that are provided in a country during the course of a year, divided by the number of people who live in the country. The amount is always worked out in US dollars so that a comparison can be made with other countries. The higher the GNI, the more developed a country will be.

2. Percentage of people employed in primary activities

The percentage breakdown of jobs within each of the employment sectors can indicate development. A rich, more developed country is likely to have:
- more people working in the secondary, tertiary and quaternary sectors.
- a low number of people working in primary activities such as agriculture.

Primary activities are those jobs or economic activities where people are involved with collecting and working with raw materials or resources (e.g. farming/agriculture, mining, quarrying and fishing).

Secondary activities are those jobs where people are involved in manufacturing or making something (e.g. iron, bread and fizzy drinks) using the raw materials collected in the primary industry.

Tertiary activities are those jobs where people provide a service to others, (e.g. doctors, lawyers, teachers and hairdressers).

Quaternary activities are when people are involved in the research and development of new products. They mostly feature in the information technology industries.

* Increasingly the term GNI (Gross National Income) is being used to replace GNP (Gross National Product).

2C: CONTRASTS IN WORLD DEVELOPMENT

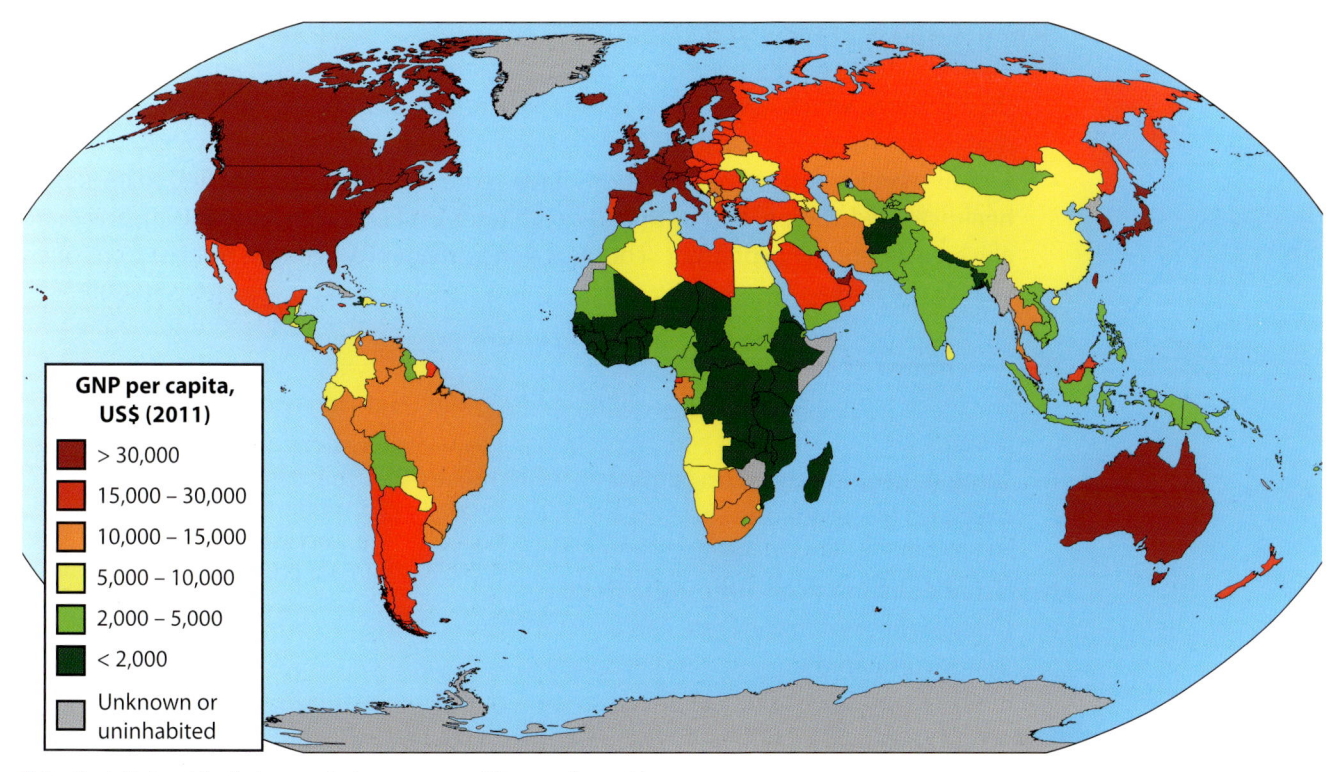

GNP per capita, US$ (2011)
- \> 30,000
- 15,000 – 30,000
- 10,000 – 15,000
- 5,000 – 10,000
- 2,000 – 5,000
- < 2,000
- Unknown or uninhabited

Using Gross National Product per capita to measure wealth across the world
Source: Data from World Bank

Country	Rank	GNI $
Qatar	1	100,450
Bermuda	2	91,950
Luxembourg	3	83,230
Norway	4	82,840
Ireland	5	79,370

Country	Rank	GNI $
Somalia	181	1,240
Congo, Dem. Rep.	182	1,110
South Sudan	183	1,040
Central African Republic	184	980
Burundi	185	780

The five richest and five poorest countries as measured by GNI, 2021
Source: Data from International Comparison Program database, World Bank | World Development Indicators database, World Bank | Eurostat-OECD PPP Programme.

Evaluate the use of social and economic indicators of development and assess the advantages of using the Human Development Index (HDI)

Evaluation of social and economic indicators
Social indicators (such as life expectancy and adult literacy rate) and economic indicators (such as Gross National Income) might be seen as being weak on their own.

Positive points of social indicators
- Life expectancy and infant mortality rates are both indicators that can be worked out easily using basic statistics collected in a country. They require information such as birth rates, death rates and age of deaths to be collected and recorded accurately.
- These indicators are used by agencies such as the United Nations and the World Health Organisation to compare investment in healthcare between countries.

Negative points of social indicators
- Many countries do not have good methods of recording the birth and death rates in their country, which means their results are not accurate. There are still many LEDCs that do not have vital registration systems in place to collect this information.
- Global charities and aid organisations have spent a lot of money helping to improve healthcare, education, and birth and death rates in LEDCs. However, this means that any investment in hospitals or schools is done privately and might not last from one year to the next.

Positive points of economic indicators
- GNI helps to give an average amount of money (in US dollars) per head of population that is earned within a country.
- Using dollars as a common currency for GNI means that comparisons between countries are easy to make.

Negative points of economic indicators
- Changes in the currency rate can affect the GNI – $1 in one country can buy different things compared to $1 in another country.
- It has become increasingly difficult to work out where the money earned in a country has come from, as many companies have bases around the world. Many company headquarters are located in MEDCs while the factories making the products are found in LEDCs (e.g. Apple's headquarters are in Cupertino in the USA but most of its devices are assembled in China.)

The advantages of using the Human Development Index (HDI)

> **Key geographical term**
>
> **The Human Development Index (HDI):** A measure of development, used by the United Nations, which combines indicators of life expectancy, educational attainment and income into a composite measure (of both social and economic indicators).

The HDI sets a minimum and maximum value for each dimension, called goalposts. It then shows where each country stands in relation to these goalposts as a value between 0 and 1, with 0 indicating minimum development and 1 maximum development.

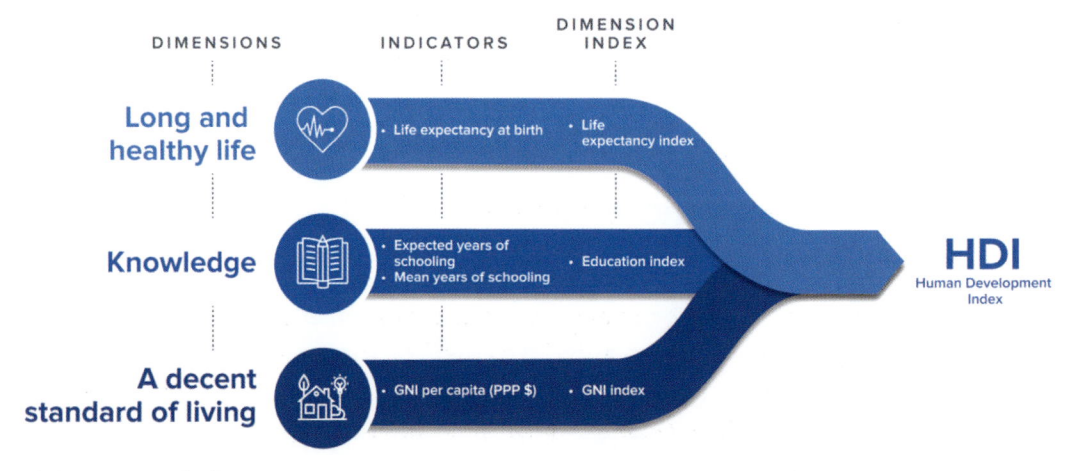

HDI Dimensions and Indicators

Source: HDI Dimensions and Indicators, © 2023 United Nations Development Programme, https://hdr.undp.org/data-center/human-development-index#/indicies/HDI

2C: CONTRASTS IN WORLD DEVELOPMENT

The HDI measures health (life expectancy at birth), education (the mean years of schooling for adults up to the age of 25 and the expected years of schooling) and the living standards (Gross National Income per capita).

Country in rank order		Human Development Index (HDI) value	Life expectancy (years)	Mean years of schooling (years)	Expected years of schooling (years)	GNI per capita (US$)
1	Switzerland	0.962	84.0	16.5	13.9	66,933
2	Norway	0.961	83.2	18.2	13.0	64,660
3	Iceland	0.959	82.7	19.2	13.8	55,782
4	Hong Kong, China (SAR)	0.952	85.5	17.3	12.2	62,607
5	Australia	0.951	84.5	21.1	12.7	49,238
187	Burundi	0.426	61.7	10.7	3.1	732
188	Central African Republic	0.404	53.9	8.0	4.3	966
189	Niger	0.400	61.6	7.0	2.1	1,240
190	Chad	0.394	52.5	8.0	2.6	1,364
191	South Sudan	0.385	55.0	5.5	5.7	768

Top and bottom 5 Countries (Very High and Low Human Development, 2021)

Source: Annex Table 1 – Human Development Index and its Components, Human Development Report 2021-22, 'Uncertain Times, Unsettled Lives: Shaping our Future in a Transforming World', © 2023 United Nations Development Programme, https://hdr.undp.org/content/human-development-report-2021-22

Positive points of the HDI
- HDI uses both economic and social data, and the most up to date figures for health (life expectancy), education (years of schooling) and GNI to create a comparison between countries.
- As HDI uses two social indicators and one economic indicator, it is more accurate and reliable.
- HDI information is updated each year, which means it is current and that countries can move up and down the index each year. Countries can look to see if they are making progress or dropping down the list.

Negative points of the HDI
- Wealth is seen as the most important element within the HDI and many development agencies argue that it is given too much importance within the HDI framework.
- Some argue that the HDI is too straightforward a measure of development. The GNI will also impact the life expectancy and education factors. The more money that a country has, the more money it can spend on schools and hospitals, which also improves the life expectancy and the mean years of schooling figures.

> ### Test your revision
> 1. What is the 'development gap'?
> 2. Describe how one social indicator might be used to measure development.
> 3. Describe how one economic indicator might be used to measure development.
> 4. Describe how the Human Development Index (HDI) measures development.
> 5. Assess the advantages of the Human Development Index (HDI) in measuring development.

> ### Revision tip
> It is easy to get confused when talking about the various measures of development. Make sure that you are clear about which are social, economic and composite measures of development.

The factors that hinder development in LEDCs

1. Historical factors
Colonial history has had an important impact on the development of many places across the world. Being part of a European Empire brought advantages (e.g. trade) but also many disadvantages. The rulers could force their subjects to fight in their armies, tax them and take their main assets (e.g. mineral wealth and land). This led to some African countries (e.g. Kenya, Democratic Republic of the Congo and Somalia) not developing as quickly as they would like.

2. Environmental factors
Environmental issues can cause people who are already poor to struggle further and put them at greater risk than people who live in MEDCs:

a. Natural hazards
The impact of natural hazards is often greater in LEDCs, as they do not have the money to plan for hazards or cope with their aftermath. For example, the 2010 earthquake in Haiti made some very poor people even poorer.

b. Extreme climates
Although many countries experience extreme climates, LEDCs often feel their impact more. In Ethiopia and Somali, droughts have made it difficult to grow food, which has led to famine and starvation. Hurricanes and flooding can pollute the land and wash the little good soil there is away. Recent climate change is also increasing the number of extreme climate events, which is putting LEDCs under even more pressure.

c. Natural resources
Much of the farmland in LEDCs can be marginal, making it difficult for farmers to produce a good yield. Water supplies can also be limited, making it difficult for people to survive. In Kenya, deep wells need to be dug to ensure that there is enough water to go around.

3. Dependence of primary activities
Countries that have some sort of mineral wealth (e.g. iron ore) or energy resources (e.g. coal, oil or natural gas) are more likely to develop industrially. This means that countries move from a dependence on primary activities (e.g. agriculture) to a

dependence on secondary activities (e.g. manufacturing). Many LEDCs continue to depend on selling their primary resources to make money, which means that they remain relatively poor. Global trade systems ensure that raw materials are processed in MEDCs so that they can maximise the profit of the finished product.

4. Debt

Many LEDCs need investment in order to make improvements to infrastructure (e.g. railway lines, hospitals and schools). As the countries cannot afford to raise the money themselves, some borrow money from other wealthier countries and international organisations. Any money borrowed must be paid back with interest and often takes a very long time to pay off. The money tied up in paying off debts cannot be used to fund further development projects. Some West African countries (e.g. the Democratic Republic of the Congo and Namibia) took out large loans with European countries that nearly crippled them financially.

> **Test your revision**
>
> 1. Describe how historical factors might hinder the development of an LEDC.
> 2. Explain the impact that environmental factors might have on development in an LEDC.
> 3. How can a dependence on primary activities be a negative influence within an LEDC?

Part 2: Sustainable solutions to the problem of unequal development

How do three of the Sustainable Development Goals attempt to reduce the development gap?

On 25 September 2015, the United Nations launched the Sustainable Development Goals (SDGs) which were part of the Agenda for Sustainable Development. The SDGs are a set of targets, agreed by the United Nations, aimed at ending poverty around the world, helping protect the planet and ensuring a new prosperity for everyone. The 17 SDGs (or the 'Global Goals') included over 169 separate targets. It was hoped that these would help to reduce the development gap and protect the planet.

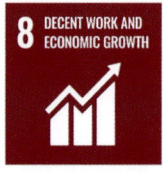

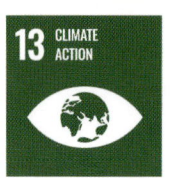

STUDY MATERIAL

SUSTAINABLE DEVELOPMENT GOALS

The Sustainable Development Goals ('Global Goals')

Source: Text of the Goals and targets, and the SDGs poster are reproduced with permission of the United Nations Sustainable Development Goals, https://www.un.org/sustainabledevelopment/

The content of this publication has not been approved by the United Nations and does not reflect the views of the United Nations or its officials or Member States.

The 17 Sustainable Development Goals icons:
1. No Poverty
2. Zero Hunger
3. Good Health and Well-being
4. Quality Education
5. Gender Equality
6. Clean Water and Sanitation
7. Affordable and Clean Energy
8. Decent Work and Economic Growth
9. Industry, Innovation and Infrastructure
10. Reduced Inequalities
11. Sustainable Cities and Communities
12. Responsible Consumption and Production
13. Climate Action
14. Life Below Water
15. Life on Land
16. Peace, Justice and Strong Institutions
17. Partnerships for the Goals

The Sustainable Development Goals ('Global Goals')

Goal 1	End poverty in all its forms everywhere.	**Goal 10**	Reduce inequality within and among countries.
Goal 2	End hunger, achieve food security and improved nutrition and promote sustainable agriculture.	**Goal 11**	Make cities and human settlements inclusive, safe, resilient and sustainable.
Goal 3	Ensure healthy lives and promote well-being for all at all ages.	**Goal 12**	Ensure sustainable consumption and production patterns.
Goal 4	Ensure inclusive and equitable quality education and promote lifelong learning opportunities for all.	**Goal 13**	Take urgent action to combat climate change and its impacts.
Goal 5	Achieve gender equality and empower all women and girls.	**Goal 14**	Conserve and sustainably use the oceans, seas and marine resources for sustainable development.
Goal 6	Ensure availability and sustainable management of water and sanitation for all.	**Goal 15**	Protect, restore and promote sustainable use of terrestrial ecosystems, sustainably manage forests, combat desertification, and halt and reverse land degradation and halt biodiversity loss.
Goal 7	Ensure access to affordable, reliable, sustainable and modern energy for all.	**Goal 16**	Promote peaceful and inclusive societies for sustainable development, provide access to justice for all and build effective, accountable and inclusive institutions at all levels.
Goal 8	Promote sustained, inclusive and sustainable economic growth, full and productive employment and decent work for all.	**Goal 17**	Strengthen the means of implementation and revitalise the Global Partnership for Sustainable Development.
Goal 9	Build resilient infrastructure, promote inclusive and sustainable industrialisation, and foster innovation.		

Note: *In this book we look at three Sustainable Development Goals but these might be different from the ones that your teacher covers in class.*

2C: CONTRASTS IN WORLD DEVELOPMENT

Goal 1: End poverty in all its forms everywhere
Economic growth must be inclusive to provide sustainable jobs and promote equality.

Global poverty rates improved between 2000 and 2015, however 1 in 10 people in LEDCs still live with their families on less than $1.90 per day. 42% of people in Sub-Saharan Africa live below the poverty line.

> **Key facts:**
> - 783 million people live below the poverty line of $1.90 per day.
> - In 2016, nearly 10% of the world's workers lived on less that $1.90 per day.
> - Most people who live below the poverty line live in Southern Asia or Sub-Saharan Africa.
> - High poverty rates are usually found in places where there is conflict.
> - 1 in 4 children aged under 5 years old are smaller in height for their age.

> **Goal 1 targets**

1.1 By 2030, eradicate extreme poverty for all people everywhere, currently measured as people living on less than $1.25 a day.

1.2 By 2030, reduce at least by half the proportion of men, women and children of all ages living in poverty in all its dimensions according to national definitions.

1.3 Implement nationally appropriate social protection systems and measures for all, including floors, and by 2030 achieve substantial coverage of the poor and the vulnerable.

1.4 By 2030, ensure that all men and women, in particular the poor and the vulnerable, have equal rights to economic resources, as well as access to basic services, ownership and control over land and other forms of property, inheritance, natural resources, appropriate new technology and financial services, including microfinance.

1.5 By 2030, build the resilience of the poor and those in vulnerable situations and reduce their exposure and vulnerability to climate-related extreme events and other economic, social and environmental shocks and disasters.

1.A Ensure significant mobilisation of resources from a variety of sources, including through enhanced development cooperation, in order to provide adequate and predictable means for developing countries, in particular least developed countries, to implement programmes and policies to end poverty in all its dimensions.

1.B Create sound policy frameworks at the national, regional and international levels, based on pro-poor and gender-sensitive development strategies, to support accelerated investment in poverty eradication actions.

> **Progress of Goal 1 in 2019**
> Extreme poverty has reduced since 1990, but pockets of poverty continue around the world. Ending poverty requires universal social protection systems aimed at safeguarding all individuals throughout the life cycle. Measures are also required to prepare for natural disasters.

- The rate of extreme poverty has fallen rapidly: in 2013 it was a third of the 1990 value. The latest global estimate suggests that 11% of the world population, or 783 million people, lived below the extreme poverty threshold in 2013.
- The proportion of the world's workers living with their families on less than $1.90 per person a day declined significantly over the past two decades, falling from 26.9% in 2000 to 9.2% in 2017.
- In 2017, economic losses attributed to disasters were estimated at over $300 billion. This is among the highest losses in recent years, owing to three major hurricanes affecting the United States of America and several countries across the Caribbean.

Goal 2: End hunger, achieve food security and improved nutrition and promote sustainable agriculture

The food and agriculture sector offers key solutions for development, and is central for hunger and poverty eradication.

The UN argue that it is time to rethink how we grow, share and consume food so that rural development is supported and the environment is protected. Climate change has been putting increased pressure on the resources that we depend on. Changes are needed to make sure that everyone has sufficient food and nourishment.

> Key facts:
- 1 in 9 people around the world (815 million) are undernourished.
- The majority of the world's hungry people live in LEDCs where nearly 13% of people are undernourished.
- Asia is the most undernourished region (with 281 million people).
- Poor nutrition causes nearly half of the deaths of children who die under the age of 5 (3.1 million children each year).
- Agriculture is the biggest employer in the world – providing work for over 40% of the global population.

> Goal 2 targets

2.1 By 2030, end hunger and ensure access by all people, in particular the poor and people in vulnerable situations, including infants, to safe, nutritious and sufficient food all year round.

2.2 By 2030, end all forms of malnutrition, including achieving, by 2025, the internationally agreed targets on stunting and wasting in children under 5 years of age, and address the nutritional needs of adolescent girls, pregnant and lactating women and older persons.

2.3 By 2030, double the agricultural productivity and incomes of small-scale food producers, in particular women, indigenous peoples, family farmers, pastoralists and fishers, including through secure and equal access to land, other productive resources and inputs, knowledge, financial services, markets and opportunities for value addition and non-farm employment.

2.4 By 2030, ensure sustainable food production systems and implement resilient agricultural practices that increase productivity and production, that help maintain ecosystems, that strengthen capacity for adaptation to climate change, extreme weather, drought, flooding and other disasters and that progressively improve land and soil quality.

2.5 By 2020, maintain the genetic diversity of seeds, cultivated plants and farmed and domesticated animals and their related wild species, including through soundly managed and diversified seed and plant banks at the national, regional and international levels, and promote access to and fair and equitable sharing of benefits arising from the utilisation of genetic resources and associated traditional knowledge, as internationally agreed.

2.A Increase investment, including through enhanced international cooperation, in rural infrastructure, agricultural research and extension services, technology development and plant and livestock gene banks in order to enhance agricultural productive capacity in developing countries, in particular least developed countries.

2.B Correct and prevent trade restrictions and distortions in world agricultural markets, including through the parallel elimination of all forms of agricultural export subsidies and all export measures with equivalent effect, in accordance with the mandate of the Doha Development Round.

2.C Adopt measures to ensure the proper functioning of food commodity markets and their derivatives and facilitate timely access to market information, including on food reserves, in order to help limit extreme food price volatility.

> **Progress of Goal 2 by 2019**

For many years, world hunger was in decline but it seems that it is on the rise again. Conflict, droughts and natural disasters have increased the number of people who are undernourished.
- The percentage of undernourished people globally increased from 10.6% in 2015 to 11.0% in 2016. This is an increase of 38 million people to 815 million.
- In 2017, 151 million children suffered low height for their age.
- Aid to agriculture in LEDCs totalled $12.5 billion in 2016. This is equivalent to 6% of all aid received compared to 19% in the mid-1980s.
- In 2016, 26 countries experienced high food prices which impacted food security.

Goal 3: Ensure healthy lives and promote well-being for all at all ages
Ensuring healthy lives and promoting the well-being for all at all ages is essential to sustainable development

Medical advances have meant that life expectancy has been increased and common killers linked to child and maternal mortality have been reduced. Further advances in reducing the number of maternal deaths and the number of premature deaths due to other communicable diseases require further effort.

STUDY MATERIAL

> **Key facts:**
> *Child health*
> - 17,000 fewer children die each day than in 1900 but 5 million children still die before their 5th birthday each year.
> - Since 2000, measles vaccines have stopped nearly 16 million deaths.
> - Children who are born into poverty are still twice as likely to die before the age of 5 than those from wealthy families.
>
> *Maternal health*
> - Maternal mortality (death during childbirth) has fallen 37% since 2000.
> - More women are getting access to antenatal care. In LEDCs access to care increased from 65% in 1990 to 83% in 2012.
>
> *HIV/AIDS, malaria and other diseases*
> - Nearly 37 million people globally were living with HIV in 2017.
> - 22 million people were able to access antiretroviral drugs in 2017.
> - 940,000 people died from AIDS-related illnesses in 2017.
> - HIV is the leading cause of death for women aged 16–50 across the world.
> - Over 6 million malaria deaths have been avoided between 2000 and 2015. The rates of people having malaria have reduced by 37% and the mortality rate has reduced by 58%.

> Goal 3 targets

3.1 By 2030, reduce the global maternal mortality ratio to less than 70 per 100,000 live births.

3.2 By 2030, end preventable deaths of newborns and children under 5 years of age, with all countries aiming to reduce neonatal mortality to at least as low as 12 per 1,000 live births and under-5 mortality to at least as low as 25 per 1,000 live births.

3.3 By 2030, end the epidemics of AIDS, tuberculosis, malaria and neglected tropical diseases and combat hepatitis, water-borne diseases and other communicable diseases.

3.4 By 2030, reduce by one third premature mortality from non-communicable diseases through prevention and treatment and promote mental health and well-being.

3.5 Strengthen the prevention and treatment of substance abuse, including narcotic drug abuse and harmful use of alcohol.

3.6 By 2020, halve the number of global deaths and injuries from road traffic accidents.

3.7 By 2030, ensure universal access to sexual and reproductive health-care services, including for family planning, information and education, and the integration of reproductive health into national strategies and programmes.

3.8 Achieve universal health coverage, including financial risk protection, access to quality essential health-care services and access to safe, effective, quality and affordable essential medicines and vaccines for all.

3.9 By 2030, substantially reduce the number of deaths and illnesses from hazardous chemicals and air, water and soil pollution and contamination.

3.A Strengthen the implementation of the World Health Organization Framework Convention on Tobacco Control in all countries, as appropriate.

3.B Support the research and development of vaccines and medicines for the communicable and noncommunicable diseases that primarily affect developing countries, provide access to affordable essential medicines and vaccines, in accordance with the Doha Declaration on the TRIPS Agreement and Public Health, which affirms the right of developing countries to use to the full the provisions in the Agreement on Trade Related Aspects of Intellectual Property Rights regarding flexibilities to protect public health, and, in particular, provide access to medicines for all.

3.C Substantially increase health financing and the recruitment, development, training and retention of the health workforce in developing countries, especially in least developed countries and small island developing States.

3.D Strengthen the capacity of all countries, in particular developing countries, for early warning, risk reduction and management of national and global health risks

> **> Progress of Goal 3 by 2019**
> Globally, people are much healthier than they have been in the past but there are still many people who are suffering due to preventable diseases.
> - From 2000 to 2016 the under-5 mortality rate has dropped by 47% (to 5.6 million).
> - In Sub-Saharan Africa the maternal mortality rate has reduced by 35% and the under-5 mortality rate has dropped by 50%.
> - The number of cases of HIV has been on the decline in recent years.
> - In 2016, 216 million cases of malaria were reported compared to 210 million cases in 2013.
> - Unsafe drinking water/sanitation caused 870,000 deaths in 2016.

Appropriate technology

> ★ **Key geographical term**
>
> **Appropriate technology:** Technology suited to the needs, skills, knowledge, resources and wealth of local people.

Often in LEDCs, hi-tech solutions to problems are inappropriate for the inhabitants as they do not have easy access to energy sources or replacement parts. Appropriate technology will provide an innovation that is suitable for the local people.

Describe and evaluate the success of one appropriate technology product (e.g. Hippo Water Roller)

The Hippo Roller

The Hippo Roller was invented in 1991 by two South Africans (Pettie Petzer and Johan Jonker) to help make water more accessible to women and children living in rural Africa. The roller is made up of a 90-litre plastic water carrier that can be rolled along the ground using a metal handle – taking away the effort of carrying water long distances. The UN World Food Program (WFP) noted that, "The introduction of Hippo rollers in WFP supported primary schools significantly reduced the daily burden on women and children for collection of water".

Image courtesy of Hippo Roller

STUDY MATERIAL

What problem does it solve?
Many people who live in rural Africa do not have good access to clean water supplies. 1.2 billion people live in areas where water resources are scarce. In Africa, 40% of households do not have access to piped-in water. People have to walk long distances with buckets and jerry cans on their heads. This can have long-term impacts on their health, as they can develop neck and spinal injuries. Children are left with the task of collecting this water, keeping them away from school, or women collect the water, which leaves them no time to make money.

Advantages
- Each roller is equal to five buckets of water, which speeds up water collection. This gives people more time for education or employment.
- The 90kg drum weighs just 10kg when rolled on level ground. It is much easier for people to move than buckets and does not put pressure on their spines and necks.
- The large opening means that it can be easily cleaned and will store water hygienically.
- In 2018 a new screw cap was added to help small-scale farmers irrigate their land. It uses a standard soda bottle top lid.
- The drum is made with thick plastic that should last between 5 and 10 years.
- The design should be maintenance-free but also comes with a selection of backup parts to help extend the roller's life.

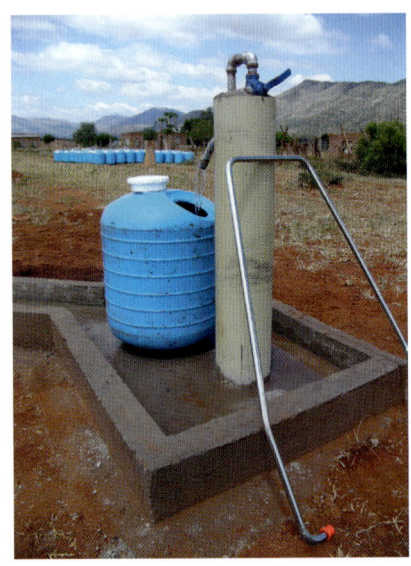

Image courtesy of Hippo Roller

However, there are also some disadvantages
- The Hippo Roller costs $200 (including distribution), so users rely on getting rollers from NGOs and charities.
- The rollers don't stack as easily as square or collapsible containers.
- The women and children still have to walk long distances to fetch water. It just makes this process a little easier.
- Some argue it would be better to spend money on creating better access to clean drinking water or digging wells.

> ⭐ **Revision tip**
>
> When studying development, it can be easy to concentrate only on key words and definitions, so make sure that you know how to evaluate the positives and negatives of some of the issues (of the use of appropriate technology).

Fair trade and the advantages it brings to LEDCs

> ⭐ **Key geographical term**
>
> **Fair trade:** A strategy used to provide an organised approach to help producers in LEDCs gain better trading conditions.

The world is not based on providing a fair system of trade, where producers can get a fair deal on all that they sell. Fair trade helps workers who were previously not treated well or paid enough for their labour get a fair price for their efforts. For many years MEDC producers and retailers have received a much better deal than producers in LEDCs.

The fair trade movement tries to make some aspects of trade fairer. The strategy aims to help producers in LEDCs get better trading conditions and promotes sustainability. The organisation is keen to ensure that producers get paid a higher price and actively promote higher social and environmental standards.

Fairtrade products are now common on shelves in supermarkets across the UK and within MEDC supply chains. These products have been imported by Fairtrade organisations or the suppliers have applied for a 'product certification' where the products have to comply with the Fairtrade production guidelines.

Why is fair trade good for producers?

1. **Fair and stable prices:** For Fairtrade products, buyers have to pay the Fairtrade minimum price. This price is good for producers as it aims to cover the costs of sustainable production and means that when the market price falls below a sustainable level, farmers do not lose out. For example, coffee prices in Colombia are now much more stable than they used to be.
2. **Fair trade for development:** Producers are also paid a Fairtrade premium, which is an extra amount paid beyond the price of the goods that the producer can spend on whatever they want. For example, Cafédirect paid a Fairtrade premium to some banana growers in Costa Rica to help purchase new equipment.
3. **Empowering small-scale farmers:** Fairtrade was set up to help empower the small-scale farmer. In some products, Fairtrade not only certifies small farmer organisations but also aims to protect the environment in a sustainable manner. In Kenya, farmers with small farms were able to band together into a collective to demand a higher price for their local-grown tea.

Fair trade coffee from Colombia

Coffee is a great example of a product where fair trade has made a real difference. Back in 1998, many coffee producers were struggling to produce coffee and make enough money to survive. Coffee prices were at an all-time low but the impact of fair trade means that coffee growers now get a greater percentage of the final cost of the product.

STUDY MATERIAL

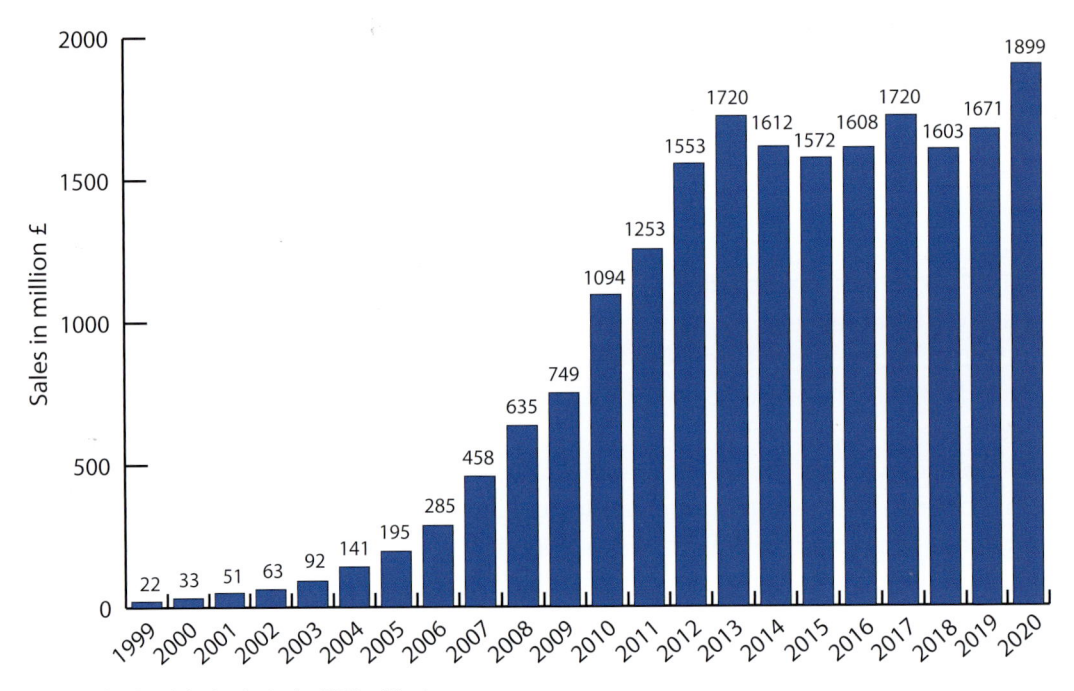

Fairtrade food and drink sales in the UK (£ million)
Source: Data from 'Sales revenue of Fairtrade food and drink products in the United Kingdom from 1999 to 2020', published by Nils-Gerrit Wunsch, www.statista.com

Year	Sales (£ million)
1999	22
2000	33
2001	51
2002	63
2003	92
2004	141
2005	195
2006	285
2007	458
2008	635
2009	749
2010	1094
2011	1253
2012	1553
2013	1720
2014	1612
2015	1572
2016	1608
2017	1720
2018	1603
2019	1671
2020	1899

★ Test your revision

1. State one Sustainable Development Goal and describe how it attempts to reduce the development gap.
2. What is 'appropriate technology'?
3. Evaluate the success of one product that uses appropriate technology.
4. Outline two reasons why fair trade can be good for producers.
5. Using the graph above, describe the trend in Fairtrade food and drink sales in the UK from 2007 to 2020.

Part 3 Globalisation

What is Globalisation?

★ Key geographical term

Globalisation: The process of the world becoming more interconnected and interdependent. People around the world are more connected to each other than ever before as jobs and industry spread across our world.

Globalisation has helped change the world in the following ways:
- Globalisation has brought the world's economies closer together (especially in relation to trade and investment).
- Trade has grown quickly between countries throughout the world, with many LEDCs increasing their industrial output.

2C: CONTRASTS IN WORLD DEVELOPMENT

- Communications have been a key factor in the continued growth of links across the world.
- Individual countries have become less independent than they used to be. Global firms such as Adidas, Coca-Cola and Nike can have more money and more control over decisions than some governments.

How does globalisation both help and hinder development?
(with reference to one case study from a BRICS country)

> ⭐ **Key geographical term**
>
> **BRICS:** The countries of Brazil, Russia, India, China and South Africa. These are the five main emerging markets or economies across the world.

How globalisation has…	
helped development	hindered development
1. Globalisation creates jobs in LEDCs, giving employees a reliable source of income in formal jobs.	1. Although jobs are created in LEDCs, the rate of pay tends to be much lower than in MEDCs.
2. Often multi-national companies (MNCs) will spend money improving the social conditions and local infrastructure. Governments, keen to attract vital foreign investment, will spend money improving roads, airports and communication links.	2. Working conditions are not always good. Employees in LEDCs often have to work long hours in very poor and sometimes unsafe environments.
3. Additional revenue means that foreign investment and money is coming into the economy.	3. In reality the depth of foreign investment is minimal. All profits flow back to the headquarters in the MEDC and the LEDC does not have the same access to the wealth.
4. People will learn and develop new skills, and often receive better education.	4. There is no guaranteed job security. Many of the jobs in LEDCs are semi-skilled and easily replaced. If a company has chosen to relocate manufacturing once, there is nothing to stop them moving again to a country where more incentives are offered.
5. New skills, technology and specialist machinery will be brought into a poor country, making it more modern.	

Case Study: China
(a globalisation case study from a BRICS country)

Company:	Nike
Founded:	Oregon, USA, 1964
Shops:	1100 worldwide
Employs:	more than 1.1 million workers in 700 contract factories in 46 countries
In the 1980s:	decided to concentrate design and marketing in the USA and sub-contract production to factories in LEDCs
Working in China:	for over 40 years, with over 156,000 workers in 112 factories

Companies such as Nike and Apple are MNCs that were founded in the USA but have moved much of their manufacturing to China.

The advantages to Nike of locating their factories in China

- **Cheap labour:** Wages are low in China (sometimes as little as 50p per hour).
- **Cheap land and services:** Land for factories is less expensive than in the USA, as are electricity and transport costs.
- **Lower taxes:** The government has given incentives and charges lower taxes and rates to attract MNCs.
- **Fewer worker rights:** Employees are not allowed to join unions, take paid holidays or receive sick pay, and can be made redundant much more easily than employees in MEDCs.

How globalisation has helped development in China

The advantages to China of companies such as Nike locating their factories in China:
- Investment by Nike and Apple helps the Chinese economy, brings better jobs and often a better standard of employment and living.
- Facilitating global companies such as Nike has led to improvements in the services and infrastructure within China, as global companies require global transport and communication links.
- Nike claims that it has been instrumental in improving working conditions for employees within China, enhancing regulations for fire safety, air quality, minimum wages and overtime limits.
- Nike locating its factories in China will attract other MNCs who are looking for new production bases. Apple based their factories in similar places, as it knew there was a skilled and reliable workforce.

How globalisation has hindered development in China

The disadvantages to China of MNCs (such as Nike) locating their factories in China:
- Typical wages in Chinese factories are low on a global scale (especially compared to those in MEDC countries). Someone doing the same job in a different part of the world would get paid more money.
- Most of the jobs are low skilled and do not require high levels of education.
- Working conditions in Chinese factories, although improving, are not universal and most workers are still working and living in conditions that are much worse than the global norm. Workers often work long hours with few breaks.
- Much of the profits generated do not go back into the Chinese economy.
- There is always the possibility that an MNC could pull out of China at any moment and take its jobs to another country that will give the company a better deal.

Test your revision

1. State the meaning of the term globalisation.
2. Describe how globalisation can help development in an LEDC.
3. What are Multinational Companies (MNCs)?
4. With reference to a case study from an LEDC, describe how globalisation has hindered development.

Theme D: Managing Our Environment

1. Human impact on the environment
2. Strategies to manage our resources
3. Sustainable tourism to preserve the environment

Part 1: Human impact on the environment

The greenhouse effect, carbon footprint and how these contribute to climate change

> **Key geographical terms**
>
> **Greenhouse effect:** The process where thermal radiation from the surface of the Earth is bounced back to the Earth due to the build-up of greenhouse gases (such as carbon dioxide and methane) in the atmosphere, causing temperatures to increase.
>
> **Carbon footprint:** The total set of greenhouse gas emissions that are caused by an organisation, event, product or person. Often this is taken as a measure of carbon dioxide emissions.
>
> **Climate change:** The long-term, global change in temperature and precipitation patterns. Many scientists believe this change has been accelerated by human activity, including the greenhouse effect.

The greenhouse effect

The greenhouse effect is a process where thermal radiation from the surface of the Earth is bounced back to the Earth due to the build-up of greenhouse gases (such as water vapour, carbon dioxide, methane, nitrous oxide, Chlorofluorocarbons (CFCs) and ozone) in the atmosphere. As a result, the temperature that surrounds the atmosphere increases.

4. The greenhouse gases that are in the atmosphere trap this infra-red (IR) radiation and the heat is reflected back towards the Earth.

1. The sun gives off energy in the form of visible light and ultra-violet (UV) radiation, which travels towards the Earth.

3. Some of the heat energy from the Earth is reflected (by seas and lakes) back into space.

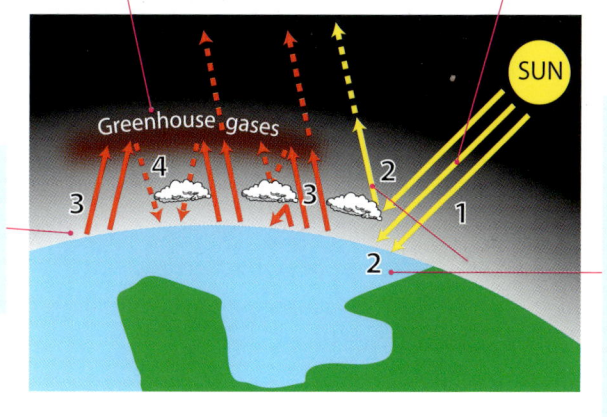

2. Some of the energy is absorbed by the atmosphere, some is absorbed by the Earth and some is reflected by clouds back into space. The rest of the energy helps to heat the surface of the Earth.

How greenhouse gases help keep the Earth warmer than normal

Global warming

Global warming is a process which causes the average temperature around the Earth to rise. The greenhouse effect is one reason for this temperature rise but there are also other causes. The Intergovernmental Panel on Climate Change (IPCC) indicated in 2007 that during the twenty-first century, the global surface temperature is likely to rise between 1.1°C to a possible 6.4°C. In 2022, the IPCC updated this and noted that global warming was likely to reach 1.5°C between 2030 and 2052.

Carbon footprint

The carbon footprint recognises that every action people take has an environmental consequence. As people use particular resources, they produce greenhouse gases through the transportation, storage and presentation of products. The total set of greenhouse gas emissions caused by each person, organisation, event or product is known as the carbon footprint.

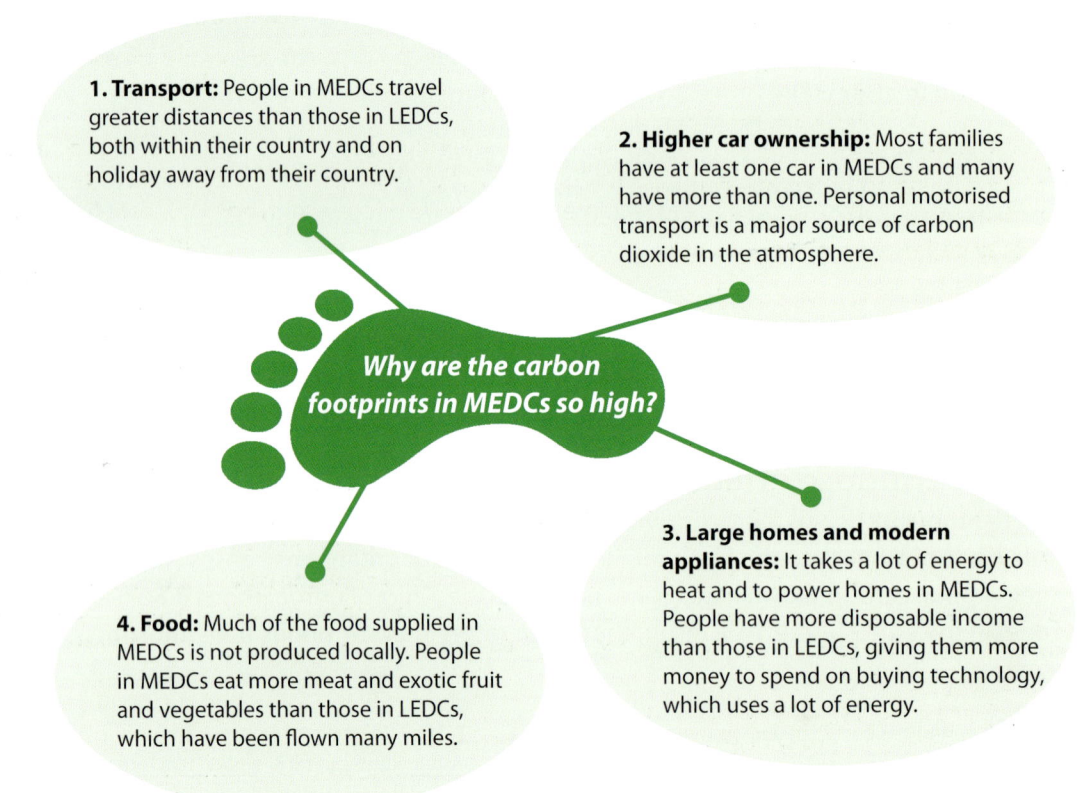

Why are the carbon footprints in MEDCs so high?

1. Transport: People in MEDCs travel greater distances than those in LEDCs, both within their country and on holiday away from their country.

2. Higher car ownership: Most families have at least one car in MEDCs and many have more than one. Personal motorised transport is a major source of carbon dioxide in the atmosphere.

3. Large homes and modern appliances: It takes a lot of energy to heat and to power homes in MEDCs. People have more disposable income than those in LEDCs, giving them more money to spend on buying technology, which uses a lot of energy.

4. Food: Much of the food supplied in MEDCs is not produced locally. People in MEDCs eat more meat and exotic fruit and vegetables than those in LEDCs, which have been flown many miles.

Evaluate the effects of climate change

Currently one of the most controversial areas in geography is the possible effects of climate change. A majority of scientists recognise that human activity has accelerated the process of global climate change. The IPCC have noted that "Taken as a whole, the range of published evidence indicates that the net damage costs of climate change are likely to be significant and to increase over time".

Effect of climate change on the environment

Effects	Positives	Negatives
Increasing temperatures The world is heating up and the rate of this increase in speeding up. Global temperatures have risen by 0.75°C over the last 100 years.	Could improve weather (and climate) in some places.	Could cause larger infestations of insects that will bring new diseases into an area.
Increasing rainfall Global rainfall patterns are changing. Places that used to be dry are experiencing more rain and wet places are experiencing long periods of drought. For example, rainfall totals in the UK and Norway are higher than 50 years ago.	Increased amount of rainfall will allow plants and crops to grow.	Although some places will have more rain, others will have less rain which will lead to drought conditions.
Glacier and icecap melt Polar icecaps and glaciers are melting at a faster rate. Some evidence shows that sea ice in the Arctic has retreated by 20%.	The polar icecaps that are traditionally frozen through the winter will not have thick ice forming all year round.	The polar bear population in the Arctic is decreasing. The bears have to swim further between flows of ice, using up more energy and causing them to lose weight and body fat. Fewer bears are surviving. Increased run-off from glaciers into rivers will cause an increase in flooding from upland areas. E.g. melting ice in Nepal will cause flooding in Bangladesh.
Sea level changes Over the last 100 years, sea levels around the UK have risen by 10cm. As water is released from storage in ice, the amount of water in the world's oceans will continue to rise (potentially up to 5m). Even a rise of 1m could flood 25% of Bangladesh.	Some coastal areas with coral reefs will have more water to help cool sea temperatures. This will allow the coral to recover from the bleaching caused by warm sea temperatures.	Flooding will cause difficulties along the coasts and lowland areas as sea levels begin to rise. This will change natural habitats and create more marsh areas.
Impact on plants and animals As changes occur to the climate, some species will be unable to adapt.	Plants will be able to be grown in new areas due to the warmer temperatures (e.g. oranges could be grown in the UK). Animals and birds will change their migration patterns to live in previously inhospitable places.	Plants will not be able to survive in some areas due to weather and climate changes (temperature and rainfall). Animals might have to migrate longer distances to find food (e.g. lions in the Savannah grasslands of Africa). Large areas of rainforest (such as the Amazon) will be lost to drought or uncontrolled fire.

Effect of climate change on people

Effects	Positives	Negatives
Food supply The impact on crops and food supply will vary across the world but as climate changes, farmers will need to change crops and farming practices. They may need to choose plants that can adapt to different climates.	Crops can be grown in new areas (e.g. grapes are now grown in some areas of southern England).	Decreased food supply and food security means that an increasing number of people are starving or malnourished (especially in Eastern African countries such as Ethiopia and Eritrea).
Availability of water If there is more rainfall in an area there may be more water available for drinking or irrigation. However, other areas might experience a higher chance of drought conditions.	The increased rainfall might increase the amount of fresh drinking water (e.g. in southern France).	The increased rainfall could build up in stagnant ponds and lakes, increasing the amount of water-borne diseases such as cholera (e.g. in India and Pakistan).
Increasing temperatures People like to go on holiday to warm countries. If temperatures continue to rise then they might not have to travel as far for a warm-weather holiday.	People might benefit from periods of warm weather in the summer and not have to travel for summer holidays.	Longer frost-free seasons will mean that fewer bugs and bacteria are killed off by the cold weather, causing an increase in deaths from diseases.
Health Changes in the atmosphere could have both good and bad impacts on health, e.g. heatwaves cause more people to end up in hospital, yet, they also allow more people to enjoy sunny days in parks or on the beach.	People will experience better health if there is a warmer climate and better weather. Warmer temperatures will allow people the chance to enjoy nature and the outdoors more.	Malnutrition will increase and more people will be endangered by extreme weather events such as drought, floods, storms, heatwaves and fires. More medical assistance will be needed to help the people affected by these events.
Mortality rates in LEDCs It is estimated that the number of deaths will increase in the future, seriously affecting 660 million people. The total cost to the global economy caused by these deaths could be nearly £220 billion per year.	Increased rainfall can lead to better crops / food supply which might help reduce death rates in LEDCs.	People in LEDCs do not have the money or resources to cope with the changes in climate. This means that even small changes to the climate could cause floods or droughts and cause more people to die.

2D: MANAGING OUR ENVIRONMENT

Effect of climate change on the economy

Effects	Positives	Negatives
Farming The length of the frost-free season will increase (and the length of the growing season). In mid-western USA it is estimated to increase by as much as 8 weeks per year. Globally, farming will have to adapt to these changes.	The amount of crops that can be grown each year will increase, which will increase the farmer's income.	Farmers will have to adapt their farming practices and ensure that they are farming the best crop for the climate that they are working in. This is easier for richer MEDC farmers (e.g. UK) – as they can afford the cost of the change of seed, animals or new machinery required – than the poorer LEDC farmers (e.g. Kenya) who have less money available.
GNI Some reports suggest that between 5–20% of global GNI will be used to prepare and protect countries from climate change.	Rich countries will be able to afford the changes needed to protect places from climate change.	It will cost countries considerable amounts of money to prepare for the effects of climate change. This will include helping many of the poorer countries (e.g. Bangladesh) prepare for flooding.
Flooding NASA predicts that global sea levels will continue to rise another 1 to 4 feet by 2100. Money will be needed to protect the coast and repair the damage caused by flooding.	Flooding will not affect countries that are inland or where there are cliffs and high land. They will benefit from changes to climate and their protected land will be worth more.	Flooding will increase in coastal areas and cities. This will damage property, businesses and factories, and will cost money to repair. A lot of money will be required to create appropriate sea defences (e.g. Egypt).
Travel Airlines have introduced levies on travellers to help reduce their carbon footprint. They will need to pay more for any pollution caused by their travel.	Transport routes in the polar ice caps are traditionally frozen through the winter but will be able to be used all year round (e.g. the North West Passage in Canada).	International travel using aircraft, boats and trains all rely on fossil fuels which causes a further increase in climate change. As more people travel, the damage done will increase.

⭐ Test your revision

1. Describe the greenhouse effect
2. Describe what a carbon footprint is.
3. Evaluate the effect of climate change on the environment.
4. Evaluate the effect of climate change on the economy.

⭐ Revision tip

The greenhouse effect and climate change are popular topics. Remember to include both positive and negative effects to support your answer when you are asked to evaluate.

STUDY MATERIAL

Part 2 Strategies to manage our resources

The waste hierarchy and the concept of 'reduce, reuse and recycle'

> ★ **Key geographical term**
>
> **Waste hierarchy:** A method used to rank waste management options in order of sustainability. Top priority goes to measures that prevent waste in the first place, followed by preparing waste for reuse, then recycling, then recovery and finally disposal.

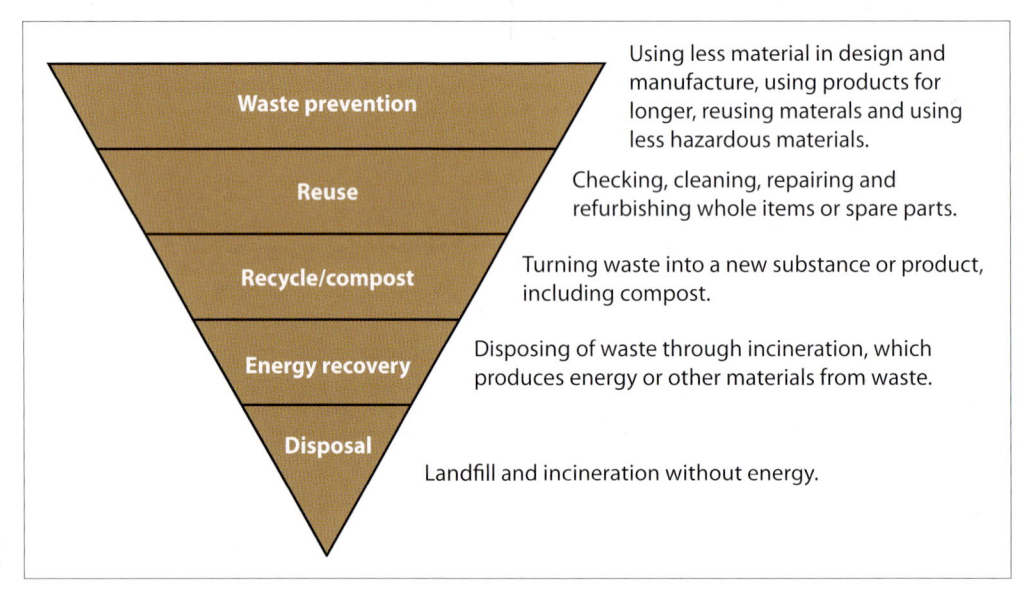

Waste prevention	Using less material in design and manufacture, using products for longer, reusing materals and using less hazardous materials.
Reuse	Checking, cleaning, repairing and refurbishing whole items or spare parts.
Recycle/compost	Turning waste into a new substance or product, including compost.
Energy recovery	Disposing of waste through incineration, which produces energy or other materials from waste.
Disposal	Landfill and incineration without energy.

The waste hierarchy

Reduce, reuse and recycle

The waste hierarchy refers directly to the idea of 'reduce, reuse, recycle'. Through this, people are encouraged to engage in activities that will have a positive environmental impact.

Reduce: encourages people to buy less and to reduce the amount of energy that they use by turning lights off, taking shorter showers, reducing food waste and the amount of packaging they use, and sharing lifts to work and school.

Reuse: encourages people to use materials again, without making them into new products, for example, reusing plastic food containers, refillable containers and fabric shopping bags. Unwanted items can be sold online, at car boot sales or given away to charity shops.

Recycle: encourages people to separate waste into component parts that can be made into new products. Energy is used to change the physical properties of the material, turning them into an alternative final product. For example, many councils in Northern

Ireland have bought park benches made from recycled plastic bottles. Upcycling is when waste materials are converted into items that are more expensive than the original article (e.g. decorating an old cabinet with modern paint colours). Downcycling is when the waste materials are converted into items that are less expensive than the original article.

Evaluate the benefits and disadvantages of one renewable energy source as a sustainable solution

> ### ★ Key geographical terms
>
> **Renewable energy source:** A sustainable source of energy production (e.g. solar, wind or biofuels). The energy can be naturally replaced and used repeatedly.
>
> **Solar energy:** A renewable energy source that uses the sun to generate power. The sun's light and heat is converted into electricity and used to heat water.
>
> **Wind energy:** A renewable energy source that uses the force of the wind to turn the sails on a turbine and generate power.
>
> **Biofuels:** Also known as biogas or biomass. A renewable energy source that uses fermented animal or plant waste to create power. Power is generated as the biological material rots and creates chemical energy.

Wind farms (a sustainable/renewable energy solution)

Wind power is a renewable energy source that uses the force of the wind to turn the sails on a turbine and generate power. In recent years, the biggest advances in wind technology have come from the UK, Denmark and California.

Walney Wind Farm is the world's largest offshore wind farm. It is located off the coast of Cumbria in the UK and opened in 2012. Its 189 wind turbines can create 1026 megawatts of energy (equivalent to supplying nearly 1 million homes).

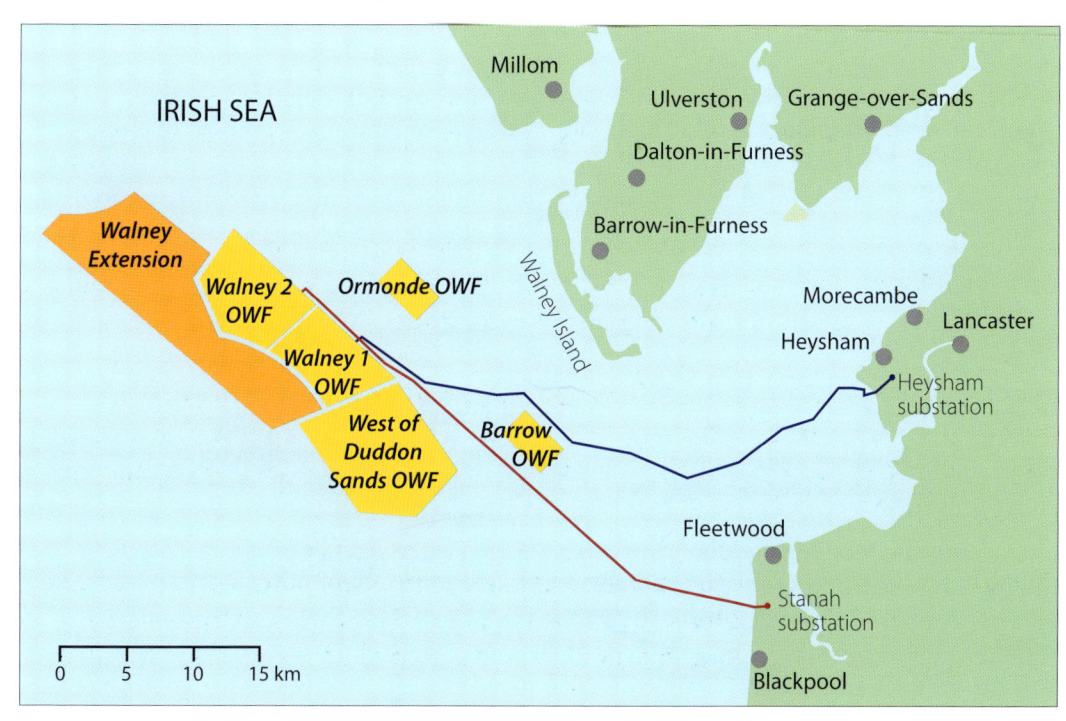

The Walney Wind Farm in the Irish Sea

STUDY MATERIAL

Wind turbines being built at Walney Wind Farm
Source: © Copyright David Dixon

Benefits of wind energy	Disadvantages of wind energy
Less carbon emissions Much of the UK's energy comes from fossil fuels that create greenhouse gases and carbon emissions. A move to a renewable source provides an inexhaustible, locally available, 'green' fuel.	**Harm to wildlife** Some scientists have concerns that the electric field created by generators in the turbines might affect the sense of direction of seals, porpoises, sharks and whales.
A source of 'green' energy Wind power is cost-effective and modern wind turbines are reliable – lasting over 20 years. The UK also has access to the most reliable wind patterns in Europe. In 2021, 26% of the energy needs of the UK came from wind power.	**Eyesores/visual impact** Some people find the wind farms ugly and feel that they will put tourists off coming to an area. However, the contractor of the Walney Wind Farm argues that it is difficult to see its wind farm as it is 14km offshore.
Reduced need for imported fossil fuels The UK has become very dependent on fossil fuels, which are mostly imported from other countries. Any reduced dependence helps the UK with its energy security.	**A need for alternative sources of energy** On calm or very windy (above 16 knots) days the turbines cannot be used. This means that a backup energy system is always needed (a non-renewable power station which can be brought to full capacity quickly).
Value for money Wind power can be expensive (especially to build) but, as fossil fuels become more expensive to use, wind power is becoming a more attractive long-term solution. Once the turbines are built, they can provide a fixed income for at least 20 years with minimal maintenance.	**High set up costs** The initial investment of £1 billion is very expensive. Wind turbines (especially those off the coast) are expensive to build and it can take over 20 years until they make a profit.

Describe and evaluate the 2015 International Climate Change Agreement

In 2015, the International Climate Change Agreement was agreed in Paris at the COP21 conference (part of the United Nations Framework Convention on Climate Change – UNFCCC). It is sometimes referred to as the 'Paris Agreement'. It was the first agreement to bring all nations together in a bid to combat climate change and greenhouse gas emissions, to adapt to the effects of climate change and to provide assistance for LEDCs.

Key points in the agreement include:
- To keep global temperatures 'well below' 2°C above pre-industrial times (and potentially below 1.5°C).
- To limit the amount of greenhouse gas emissions due to human activity so that trees, soil and oceans can naturally absorb the carbon emissions (between 2050 and 2100).
- To review the contribution that each country is making in cutting emissions every five years.
- For MEDCs to help LEDCs by providing 'climate finance', which will help poorer countries to adapt to climate change and encourage the use of renewable energy.

World leaders celebrate the signing of the 2015 International Climate Change Agreement in Paris Source: COP21 / Alamy Stock Photo

196 countries agreed to the deal and it officially came into force on 4 November 2016. Every country in the world has signed the agreement. In 2017 President Trump pulled the USA out of the deal but, on his first day in office, President Biden signed an executive order to re-join the agreement.

Positives of the Paris Agreement	Negatives of the Paris Agreement
This is the very first time that all the world leaders agreed to create any limit to global warming.	This agreement came after 36 years of climate meetings that made little progress.
World leaders also agreed to policies aiming for zero emissions in the second half of the 21st century.	The agreement is non-binding – this means that this is not a legal document and there are few penalties for countries that fail to take any action.
This is the first agreement to attempt to slow down the impacts of global warming. The agreement aims to limit global warming to "well below 2°C and striving for 1.5°C".	Environmental lobby groups like Greenpeace and Friends of the Earth argue that the agreement has not gone far enough. They note that a target of 2°C is ridiculous as it has nearly been reached already.
Some countries made early decisions to implement changes to how they act. France has already announced it will ban the sale of all petrol and diesel cars by 2040. Norway has also set a target of only allowing sales of 100% electric or plug-in hybrid cars by 2025.	Many of the different pledges within the agreement did not come into effect until 2020 (five years after the meeting).
All governments agreed to review their climate policies and success every five years. The CBI (Confederation of British Industry) noted that the Agreement was "an exciting opportunity for business".	The USA initially signed up to the agreement but President Trump removed them from the deal in 2017. It was the only country to withdraw from the agreement. In 2021, the newly-elected President Biden signed an executive order for the USA to re-join.
Some of the countries that currently produce the most pollution made commitments to cut down. China accounts for almost 24% of all global emissions and has agreed to reduce this by 60%.	Friends of the Earth Scotland were critical of the deal. They said it delays any real impact on greenhouse gas emissions and failed to commit enough finance to support poorer countries.

STUDY MATERIAL

⭐ Test your revision

1. What is the waste hierarchy?
2. Describe the concept of 'reduce, reuse and recycle'.
3. Evaluate two benefits and two disadvantages of one renewable energy source you have studied.
4. Describe the main features of the 2015 International Climate Change Agreement.
5. Evaluate the 2015 Paris International Climate Change Agreement.

⭐ Revision tip

There are many possible 'evaluate' questions in this unit. Make sure that you have a clear understanding of both the positive and negative points, before summarising your argument with a final evaluative statement. You might want to emphasise which side of the argument you find the most persuasive.

Part 3 — Sustainable tourism to preserve the environment

Evaluate the positive and negative cultural, economic and environmental impacts of mass tourism

Tourism is the temporary, short-term movement of people to destinations outside the places where they normally live and work, and activities during their stay at these destinations.

⭐ Key geographical term

Mass tourism: When large numbers of people go on holiday to the same resort, usually at the same time of year, often as part of a package deal.

Tourists enjoying the beach under an airport flight path. Maho Beach, St Martin. Image courtesy of Benny Zheng

2D: MANAGING OUR ENVIRONMENT

Tourism has become increasingly important to the economic development of countries and it has led to a number of positive and negative impacts.

	Positive impacts	**Negative impacts**
Cultural impacts of tourism	• *Revitalisation:* When tourists come to an area, this triggers a revitalisation of neglected areas, government investment and the building of new community facilities (e.g. traditional beer gardens and museums in Berlin). • *Rebirth of customs:* Tourism can cause a rebirth of local arts, craft and customs (e.g. embroidery, lace and ceramics in the Algarve in Portugal).	• *Inappropriate behaviour:* The behaviour of tourists can distort local customs and tourists can insult the culture, values and beliefs of the hosts. Crime and drunken behaviour might increase (e.g. Majorca). • *Move from traditional employment:* Traditional activities such as farming can be lost as young people seek to move into new tourism jobs (e.g. Costa del Sol). • *Loss of local languages:* Local languages can be lost through under use (e.g. Majorca).
Economic impacts of tourism	• *Creates jobs:* The UNWTO estimates that 385 million people around the world are employed in the travel and tourism industry (11% of the total workforce). • *Foreign currency:* Cash coming into a country can help it to develop and stabilise the economy (e.g. Kenya). • *Improvements to infrastructure:* If a country attempts to improve its transport, utilities and communications to attract tourists, this will also benefit inhabitants (e.g. better road networks and airports in Cyprus).	• *Services:* The services in many resorts are designed and priced to cater for the tourist. Locals may have limited access to water services, entertainment and transport, and struggle to afford the inflated prices (e.g. Majorca). • *Land and house prices:* Some tourists buy second homes which can increase the price of housing. Local people may not be able to afford the higher prices (e.g. London). • *Character changes:* Rural areas might lose their traditional characteristics. Traditional services and shops may be replaced with those that cater for the needs of the tourist. (e.g. Normandy and rural France.)
Environmental impacts of tourism	• *Sustainable tourism:* Visitors may actively participate in helping an area to be maintained and protected. • *Awareness:* Tourism to remote places can help expose the environmental problems and negative activities that are taking place there. • *Improvements:* The development of tourism can bring much needed improvements to derelict areas and tidy up clean waterways.	• *Soil erosion:* Erosion of soil, rock and vegetation can be caused by walkers and horse riders. This can damage fragile environments such as mountain areas (e.g. the Alps). • *Congestion:* Too many people visiting areas at any one time can cause overcrowding and congestion, increasing carbon emissions (e.g. Paris). • *Pollution:* Tourists can pollute water, air and cause noise. This can also put pressure on water supplies.

STUDY MATERIAL

Describe and explain how to be a responsible tourist

> ⭐ **Key geographical terms**
>
> **Sustainable tourism:** Tourism that takes full account of its current and future economic, social and environmental impacts. It addresses the needs of visitors, the industry, the environment and host communities.
>
> **Responsible tourism:** Any form of tourism where visitors do their best to minimise any negative social, environmental or economic impacts on the local people.

Often tourists are only concerned with getting the best deal possible and do not necessarily care about the impact their travel will have on local people and the local environment.

A responsible tourist will do their best to reduce any negative impact and will try to help any community that they come into contact with.

The United Nations World Tourism Organisation (UNWTO) produced a booklet called 'Tips for a responsible traveller'. In this they identify some of the different ways that travellers can ensure that they behave responsibly, such as:

Sustainable tourism

- **Honour your hosts and their common heritage**
  - Research your destination and learn about local customs and traditions.
  - Learn to speak a few words in the local language.
  - Experience what makes that destination unique – from its history, architecture, religion and dress to its music, art and cuisine.

- **Protect our planet**
  - Be a guardian of natural resources, especially forests and wetlands.
  - Respect wildlife and natural habitats.
  - Purchase products that are not linked to endangered plants or animals.
  - Reduce your water and energy consumption when possible.

- **Support the local economy**
  - Buy locally-made handcrafts and products.
  - Pay a fair price to local artisans.
  - Hire local guides.

- **Travel safely**
  - Take appropriate health and safety precautions.
  - Know how to access medical care.

- **Be an informed traveller**
  - Observe national laws and regulations.
  - Respects human rights and avoid exploitation.
  - Refrain from giving money to begging children. Support community projects instead.

Source: Adapted from 'Tips for a responsible traveller', UNWTO, https://www.unwto.org/responsible-tourist

Ecotourism

Ecotourism is described as tourism that:
- is environmentally sound.
- protects natural environments, wildlife and resources.
- is socially appropriate and respectful of local culture.
- does not damage local communities.
- provides economic benefits for local people.
- leads to sustainable tourism.

> **Key geographical term**
>
> **Ecotourism:** A sustainable type of tourism, which protects the wildlife and natural resources of the host area.

The International Ecotourism Society (TIES) defines ecotourism as: "responsible travel to natural areas that conserves the environment, sustains the well-being of the local people, and involves interpretation and education."

It goes on to describe the key principles of ecotourism:

> "Ecotourism is about uniting conservation, communities and sustainable travel. This means that those who implement, participate in and market ecotourism activities should adopt the following ecotourism principles:
>
> - Minimise physical, social, behavioural, and psychological impacts.
> - Build environmental and cultural awareness and respect.
> - Provide positive experiences for both visitors and hosts.
> - Provide direct financial benefits for conservation.
> - Generate financial benefits for both local people and private industry.
> - Deliver memorable interpretative experiences to visitors that help raise sensitivity to host countries' political, environmental, and social climates.
> - Design, construct and operate low-impact facilities.
> - Recognise the rights and spiritual beliefs of the Indigenous People in your community and work in partnership with them to create empowerment."

Source: 'What is ecotourism?', The International Ecotourism Society, https://ecotourism.org/what-is-ecotourism/

Case Study: Kenya, an LEDC
(assess how ecotourism can protect the environment, using one case study from either an LEDC or a MEDC)

Kenya was one of the first African countries to embrace mass tourism. Most of the tourists here come from Europe and stay in coastal resorts but also spend some time on safari to an inland wildlife reserve. In 2019 Kenya earned over $1.3billion from tourism.

Ecotourism resort:	The Mara Intrepids Camp
Location:	The savannah grasslands of the Maasai Mara National Reserve
Camp consists of:	30 luxury tents which are spread across a riverside

What makes this 'ecotourism'?

The Mara Intrepids Camp has received the second highest ecotourism award in Kenya – a silver award. Ecotourists here are able to travel to the Maasai Mara National Park and go on Safari to see some of the animals that live on the savannah grasslands. They are also able to find out how local people live and work in this part of Kenya.

The Mara Intrepids Camp in Kenya
Images courtesy of the Mara Intrepids Camp

2D: MANAGING OUR ENVIRONMENT

Social and economic impacts	Environmental impacts
• **Jobs:** Many of the staff at the camp are local Maasai people. This provides stable employment and a good income.	• **Wildlife conservation:** Guests are educated about wildlife conservation. Guides are trained not to disturb the animals whilst on safari drives and jeep numbers are kept to a minimum to reduce noise pollution.
• **Staff training and opportunities:** The camp gives professional training to all of its staff. First aid training is also provided.	• **Water:** Grey water (from washing) and black water (from toilets) is filtered before being released into nearby rivers.
• **Cultural visits:** The camp organises a series of cultural visits for tourists which helps to build links with the local community.	• **Electricity:** The majority of electricity is from a generator but char dust (compacted coffee husks) is used to heat water.
• **Community action:** In June 2010 the hotel teamed up with MEAK (Medical and Educational Aid to Kenya) to set up a local 'Eye Mission to the Mara' where cataract operations and eye treatments helped many of the local people.	• **Waste:** All kitchen waste is composted and other waste is recycled.
• **Supports education:** The camp supports a local primary school in Talek and provides reading and writing materials.	• **Food:** The camp has an eco-garden where it grows its own vegetables
	• **Buildings:** Many of the camp buildings are temporary and are designed to blend in with the local environment.

⭐ Test your revision

1. Evaluate some of the cultural impacts that tourism has had on an area.
2. Describe what being a responsible tourist means.
3. Define the term 'ecotourism'.
4. Assess how ecotourism can help to protect the environment with reference to a case study you have studied.

Practice Questions

Getting the best grade possible

There are three units that you must complete for your CCEA GCSE in Geography:
- **Unit 1: Understanding Our Natural World** (physical geography)
  1 hour 30 mins exam paper (40% of the overall GCSE qualification)
- **Unit 2: Living in Our World** (human geography)
  1 hour 30 mins exam paper (40% of the overall GCSE qualification)
- **Unit 3: Fieldwork**
  1 hour exam paper (20% of the overall GCSE qualification)

This student guide covers Unit 2, so the following advice focuses on the Unit 2 exam paper. However, some of the guidance could also be applied to Units 1 and 3.

Exam advice

1. What to bring with you to the exam

Bring a ruler, a pencil, a black pen, a calculator, a protractor (angle measure) and a packet of five colouring pencils with you to the exam.

2. Manage your time

You have 90 minutes (1½ hours) to sit your Unit 2 exam paper. You need to manage your time well to make sure you get it completed.

The table opposite shows how the exam paper is structured, the marks for each question, and how long you should spend on it. You will see that there is a question for each chapter of the study material in this book.

GETTING THE BEST GRADE POSSIBLE

Unit 1: Understanding Our Natural World

Question	Description	Marks (out of 100)	Exam timing (out of 90 minutes)
Q1: Theme A: Population and Migration	One multi-part question addressing population (might also include map work).	25	22½ minutes
Q2: Theme B: Changing Urban Areas	One multi-part question addressing settlement (might also include map work).	25	22½ minutes
Q3: Theme C: Contrasts in World Development	One multi-part question addressing development issues.	25	22½ minutes
Q4: Theme D: Managing Our Environment	One multi-part question addressing global warming, waste and tourism.	25	22½ minutes
Quality of Written Communication	The examiner will assess the quality of written communication of your answers to three questions on the paper.	Part of the marks allocation	Part of time allocation

3. Use the marks as a guide

Each question (1, 2, 3 and 4) is broken down into smaller parts (a, b, c, etc.).
Use the marks allocated alongside each part to help you work out how long to spend on it and how much depth you need to go into for your answer. You need to work quickly through the shorter questions so that you have more time to spend on longer response questions.

- For a question worth 7 marks you should aim to spend around 7 minutes answering it. Don't spend any longer or you won't get the paper finished in time. Keep your answers concise and get straight to the point.
- The number of lines also provides a good indication of how much you should write.

4. Answer the question asked

It is important to read each question thoroughly to make sure that you know what you are being asked to do. One of the biggest mistakes that candidates make is not answering the question asked on the exam paper. Ideally, you should read every question **three** times. On the third reading it is a good idea to circle any command or key words. If you are asked to refer to a resource or a case study, make sure that you use specific facts and details that relate to the question.

PRACTICE QUESTIONS

5. Understand the command words

Make sure that you know what the common command words mean. There is a big difference between a question that asks you to **describe** a graph and one that asks you to **explain** the trend shown on a graph.

Compare	What are the main differences and similarities?
Contrast	What are the main differences?
Describe	Give details of a known concept or case study, or use details to show the shape or pattern of a resource. What does it look like? What are the highs, lows and averages?
Discuss	Describe and explain. Argue a particular point, but you might need to address both sides of an argument (agree and disagree).
Explain	Give reasons why a pattern or feature exists using geographical knowledge.
Evaluate	Look at the positive and negative points of a particular strategy or theory and give an overall concluding statement.
Identify	Choose or select.
Outline	Set out the main characteristics. Provide a brief description or explanation as required by the question.

6. Structure your answer

If an exam question seems daunting, try breaking it down into chunks. This will help you to structure the answer fully. For example, the following question could be asked in the Unit 2 exam:

"Evaluate the benefits and disadvantages of one renewable energy source that you have studied." [7]

To answer this question, you must:

1. recognise that it is referring to one renewable energy source (such as wind farms/wind energy).

2. evaluate both sides of the source:
   a) briefly describe the details of the ONE renewable energy source.
   b) look at both the benefits and disadvantages of wind energy.
   c) provide an overall concluding statement, which clearly shows whether the use of this energy source was more a benefit or a disadvantage.

   A 7-mark question will be marked using a levels of response mark scheme. Any evaluate answer should include a balanced look at both the positives and negatives of the strategy, followed by a concluding evaluative statement.

7. If you have time at the end

If you have some time left after completing the paper, then it is important that you check through your answers and make sure that you have:
- a) answered everything, and
- b) included as much detail as possible.

Use every second to squeeze every last mark out of your paper that you can.

> **Revision tip**
>
> Your hand can be your most useful tool! Cover up your answers with your hand and ask yourself the question again. Think about what things you would expect in a good answer for this question and look under your hand to see what you wrote. Add in anything you missed.

PRACTICE QUESTIONS

Exam-style questions

The following pages provide exam-style questions and examples of student answers **in blue**. These student answers provide a basis for your own response and will be followed by some examiner tips **in red** to show how the answers could have been improved.

Theme A: Population and Migration

1. State the meaning of the term crude birth rate. [2]

   Crude birth rate is the number of live births each year.

   1/2 marks awarded
   The answer covers the first part of the definition but should indicate that these births are per thousand of the population in an area in order to get the second mark.

2. Study **Figure 1** which shows population pyramids for Germany and Turkey in 2010. Answer the question which follows.

   Figure 1
   Source: Data from U.S. Census Bureau, Public Information Office (PIO)

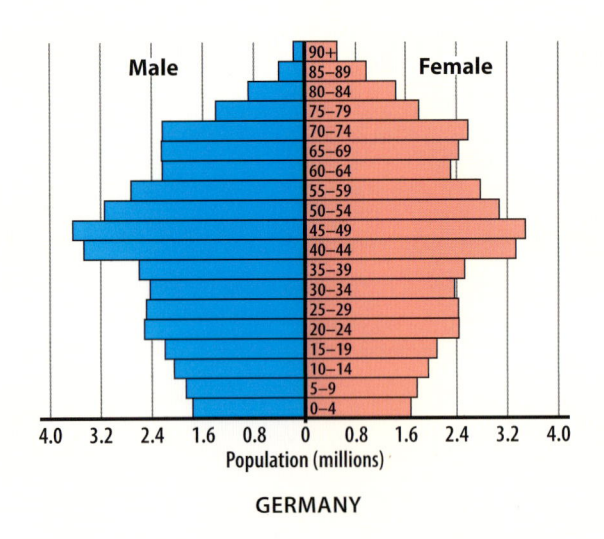

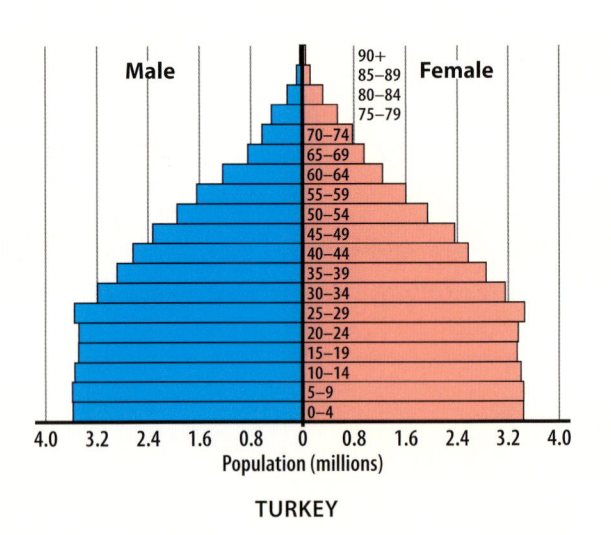

   GERMANY

   TURKEY

   Describe **two** differences between the population pyramids of Germany and Turkey. [6]

   The bottom of Turkey's pyramid is much wider than Germany's. Turkey has a larger birth rate (7 million people aged 0–4) than Germany (3.2 million people aged 0–4). Turkey also has a much higher death rate than Germany. The top of Turkey's pyramid (3 million people aged 75+) is much narrower than Germany's (over 6 million aged 75+). Therefore, Turkey shows characteristics of a youthful population while Germany shows characteristics an aged population.

5/6 marks awarded
This student has put together some good points. They compare the 0–4 age group and their description is supported through the use of accurate figures and a reference to the shape of the pyramid. The second description deals with those aged 75 and older and again is supported with appropriate facts and figures. However, the answer needs a bit more detail describing the shape of the pyramids.

There is a valid statement with detailed information and clear reference to the pyramids, such as the shape of the pyramid or the bars.

3. Study **Figure 2** which is a graph showing the demographic transition model. Answer the questions which follow.

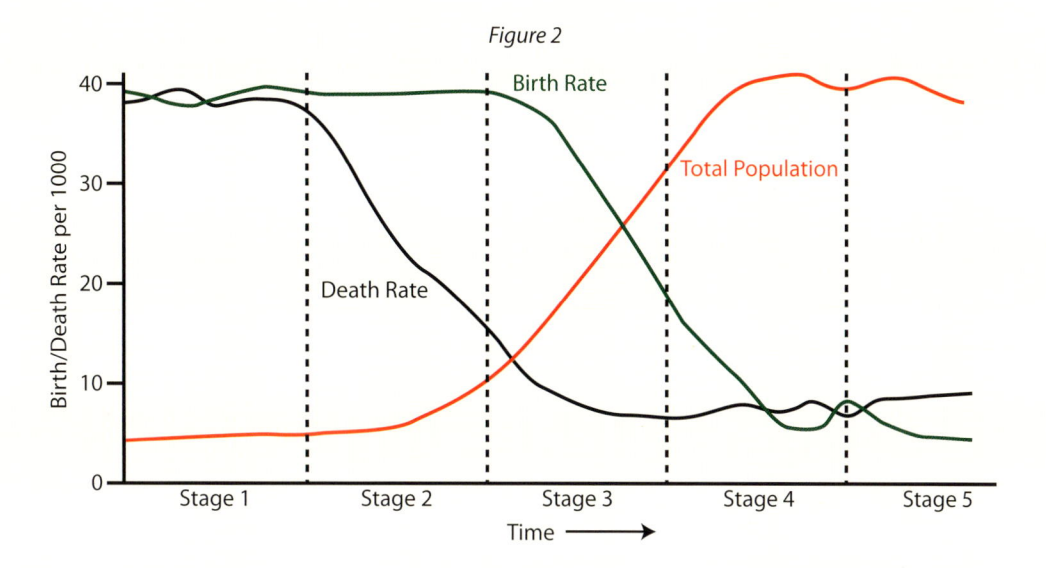

Figure 2

(a) Describe the changes to birth and death rates. [4]

> The birth rates start high (around 40/1000) in stage 1 and remain high until the start of stage 3 where they begin to drop quite quickly. By the start of stage 4 the birth rates will be about 20/1000. They will continue to decrease and eventually the birth rate will dip below the death rate to around 6/1000.
>
> The death rates also start high (around 40/1000) but are the first to drop in stage 2, and by the start of stage 3 will have dropped to about 16/1000. The death rate then stabilises and remains around 10/1000.

4/4 marks awarded
This is a full answer that shows a clear use of the figures from the graph and the stages along the bottom of the graph. The candidate has identified the main changes to both the birth rate and the death rate, and both are dealt with in some detail.

PRACTICE QUESTIONS

(b) Explain why the population continues to grow at Stage 3 of the demographic transition model. [4]

> The reason why the population grows in stage 3 of the demographic transition model is because the birth rate is still high and the death rate is low, which means there is a natural increase.

1/4 marks awarded
This answer contains a limited explanation. There is some reference to the birth rates being high but the answer needs to focus on why the death rates have dropped to a low level and why there is a widening gap between the low death rate and decreasing birth rate. This answer includes a basic statement of the changes but has not gone into enough detail to explain why these changes have been happening.

4. Describe the difference between an economic migrant and a refugee. [3]

> An economic migrant is someone who moves to change job and a refugee is someone who is trying to escape from war.

2/3 marks awarded
This answer describes the differences between an economic migrant and a refugee but both definitions require more depth. An economic migrant is someone who moves in order to improve their standard of living, wage or job prospects. This is usually seen as a pull factor as the person has a choice to move. A refugee is someone who is fleeing from events such as civil wars or natural disasters. These are push factors as the person has no choice but to move.

5. Explain the challenges faced by both refugees and the destination country, using your case study on migration. [6]

> In recent years there have been many refugees who have left Syria to move into Turkey. The civil war in Syria has been tearing the country apart. Some of the challenges that the Syrians faced in Turkey have included the fact that conditions in the refugee camps are terrible, with many people struggling to find food or water supplies. Some of the refugees have been sent back to Syria as their documentation has been called into question. Over 3 million Syrians are living in Turkey and this continues to put pressure on the Turkish people.

4/6 marks awarded
Level 1 = 1–2 marks
An answer with a basic statement of the challenges faced by refugees and/or the destination country.
Level 2 = 3–4 marks
An answer with a limited explanation of the reason with some elaboration and either explains one aspect of the question in detail or both aspects of the question in less detail.
Level 3 = 5–6 marks
An answer that provides a detailed explanation of the challenges faced by refugees and the destination country with solid evidence and information discussed in relation to relevant case study material.

EXAM-STYLE QUESTIONS

This answer provides some good detail on the challenges faced by the refugees but needs to go into more detail on the challenges faced by the destination country. Therefore this answer could only receive a high level 2 mark.

Theme B: Changing Urban Areas

6. Study the Ordnance Survey extract of Belfast (1:50,000 scale) in **Figure 3**. Answer the questions which follow.

Figure 3

This is Crown Copyright and is reproduced with the permission of Land & Property Services under delegated authority from the Controller of Her Majesty's Stationery Office, Crown copyright and database right 2023 PMLPA No 100496

(a) State the straight-line distance from the car park at Belfast Zoological Gardens at GR 326810 to the car park at the Odyssey Arena at GR 348746 [2]

6km

0/2 marks awarded

The correct answer is 6.75km. An answer between 6.65–6.85km will be awarded 2 marks with answers 6.55–6.64 or 6.86–6.95 receiving 1 mark.

73

PRACTICE QUESTIONS

(b) Part of Belfast's CBD is located in grid squares 3374 and 3474. State **two** pieces of map evidence which support this statement. [2]

> There are a lot of car parks in this area which shows that many people might drive into this area for work or shopping. Many of the roads bring traffic into the city and meet close to the CBD.

2/2 marks awarded
The student has correctly identified two pieces of map evidence. The high number of church buildings or the convergence of communications (road, rail, motorways) are both acceptable answers.

(c) Describe **one** way in which the area in grid square 3574 is typical of an inner-city area. [2]

> Many of the streets in this area are long and straight in a grid-like pattern, which probably means that the streets are terraced houses built close to factories.

2/2 marks awarded.
Award 1 mark for a basic description referring to the straight streets, long rows of buildings or a high density of buildings. Award 2 marks for a more developed description, for example, the buildings are terraced houses or this is an area just outside the area of the CBD.

There is a developed description for both marks.

(d) Study **Figure 4** which shows a photograph of the Titanic Quarter development in inner city Belfast (GR 350749). This area has recently been developed with new residential properties. Answer the questions which follow.

Figure 4

EXAM-STYLE QUESTIONS

Many newcomers have moved into the Titanic Quarter Arc development in the last few years. Using only information from the Ordnance Survey map and the photograph, explain why this inner-city area has attracted newcomers. [6]

> The inner-city area has attracted many newcomers to the area as recent property development has taken place in the new Titanic Quarter. The creation of new apartments has attracted more people into the inner-city area. The photograph shows that the apartments have been built very close to the old industrial area, as you can see the H&W (Harland and Wolff shipyard) crane in the background. The map shows that this area has been built close the industrial area of Queens Island which means that this is regeneration.

4/6 marks awarded
Levels of response are used in this question:

Level 1 = 1–2 marks
A basic answer might refer to the map or photo evidence.
- The area is close to the CBD and amenities
- It is close to major road and railway connections
- It is part of a regeneration area

Level 2 = 3–4 marks
An answer that uses evidence from both the map and the photo but with limited detail.

Level 3 = 5–6 marks
An answer that provides a detailed description about why the area might be attractive to newcomers. It must use both map and photo evidence.

This answer contains some useful detail and has attempted to use both the map and the photo. To achieve a Level 3 the student would need to go into further depth, such as the area is developing jobs, education and other services, which will encourage more people to live there, within close access of the CBD. This must be supported with specific evidence from the photo and the map.

PRACTICE QUESTIONS

(e) Figure 5 shows an aerial photograph of part of The Titanic Quarter site and the Belfast Harbour area, which is located in grid squares 3475 and 3575.

Using **map** evidence outline **two** reasons why this is a good location for an inner-city industrial zone. [4]

Figure 5

Image captured by Colin Williams Photography

> There are good transport links with wide roads, making this area good for an industrial zone as it allows the transport of heavy and large industrial machinery to and from the area. It also contains buildings that are large enough to house factories and enable industrialisation.

3/4 marks awarded
An answer will usually focus on the proximity of a good communication network or space for development. The area is close to motorway and primary routes/railway stations/Belfast port/Belfast City Airport.

Award 1–2 marks
Two basic statements or one statement with a consequence.
- Good communications
- Room to expand
- Within a large city

Award 3–4 marks
Two valid statements with elaboration that mentions specific evidence from the map.

This answer raises some good points that address the question but requires more evidence from the photo and the map. The second reason is a little vague with some reference to large factories for one mark.

EXAM-STYLE QUESTIONS

7. Evaluate the extent to which an MEDC urban planning scheme you have studied has improved transport and the environment. [6]

> In the Titanic Quarter in Belfast there has been a new regeneration strategy put into place to change the look of the city. As part of the plan, the Titanic Quarter has attempted to improve transport links with the rest of the city. New Glider buses started in 2018 and now link the area with other parts of east and west Belfast. There is also a rail link and regular buses to make sure that people can travel by public transport to their jobs/education. In addition, before the building work began a lot of money was spent cleaning up the industrial pollution on the site. The area is now a vibrant and attractive place for people to live and work.

4/6 marks awarded

Level 1 = 1–2 marks
Mentions a basic statement in relation to one of the attempts to regenerate and improve either the transport or the environment.

Level 2 = 3–4 marks
An answer that has a limited description of both aspects of the question – both transport and the environment with some limited detail and evaluation.

Level 3 = 5–6 marks
An answer that includes detailed information for all aspects of the question – looking at both transport and the environment, and contains an evaluation of both.

In this answer, the student has started to address the question and has some good information on the attempts to improve transport. There is some comment on the environment but not enough evaluation. There needs to be more reflection on the extent to which the urban planning scheme has improved both transport and the environment in the case study area for the answer to be considered as a Level 3.

8. Briefly describe **one** characteristic of a shanty town you have studied. [3]

> Shanty town is the name given to the spontaneous housing in Sao Paulo, a LEDC in Brazil. The people who live in a shanty town like Paraisopolis find it really difficult to get formal jobs. There is a lot of unemployment in Paraisopolis and people are forced to work in the informal sector or turn to crime – they might shine shoes or work as drug dealers.

3/3 marks awarded.

Award 1 = 1 mark
A basic answer that describes the characteristic in general terms.

Award 2 = 2 marks
A limited answer that describes the characteristic of the shanty town.

Award 3 = 3 marks
A detailed answer in relation to the characteristics identified (maybe employment or housing) with specific detail added.

This answer dealt comprehensively with the question. There is good description of a characteristic that would be expected within a shanty town.

PRACTICE QUESTIONS

Theme C: Contrasts in World Development

9. Study **Table 1** which shows two indicators of development for five countries. Answer the questions that follow.

Table 1

Country	Life Expectancy (years)	GNI Per capita ($)
Norway	83	64,660
Iceland	83	55,782
Zimbabwe	59	3,810
Mali	58	2,133
Congo (DR)	59	1,076

Figures from: 2022 Human Development Report, United Nations Development Programme.

Using information from the table, identify one country that might be considered an MEDC and one country that might be considered an LEDC. [2]

MEDC: __Norway__

LEDC: __Zimbabwe__

2/2 marks awarded
The candidate has correctly identified Norway as an MEDC. The other possibility was Iceland. The candidate has also identified Zimbabwe correctly as an LEDC. The other possibilities were Mali or Congo (DR).

10. The Human Development Index (HDI) often uses information such as life expectancy and GNI (per capita) to help indicate development.

(a) Name **one** other indicator that is included when calculating the Human Development Index (HDI) for a country. [1]

Years of schooling

1/1 mark awarded
The revised HDI index also uses mean years of schooling (in years) and expected years of schooling (in years) within its matrix.

(b) Explain some of the advantages of using the HDI as an indicator of development. [4]

The Human Development Index is good because it is a combination of social indicators, such as literacy rate, birth rate and years of schooling, as well as the economic indicator of gross national product. This combination gives a statistic which shows a balance of the social and economic progress of the country, leading to excellent levels of accuracy. This is why it is the most effective indicator of development, as it looks at both sides of the story and doesn't depend too much on one or the other.

3/4 marks awarded

Level 1 = 1 mark
An answer that gives a basic statement of what the HDI is.

Level 2 = 2–3 marks
A statement with limited understanding of what is involved in the HDI – that it is a composite measure including social and economic data.

Level 3 = 4 marks
A statement that shows a detailed understanding of what is involved in the discussion of HDI, with some further description of how the social and economic indicators are needed to measure the development.

In this answer the student notes that birth rate is involved, which is not the case (it is life expectancy). Otherwise the answer is strong and goes into some depth about the different indicators and why these are effective.

11. Study **Figure 6** which shows the amount of sales in millions of pounds of Fairtrade food and drink products in the UK. Answer the questions that follow.

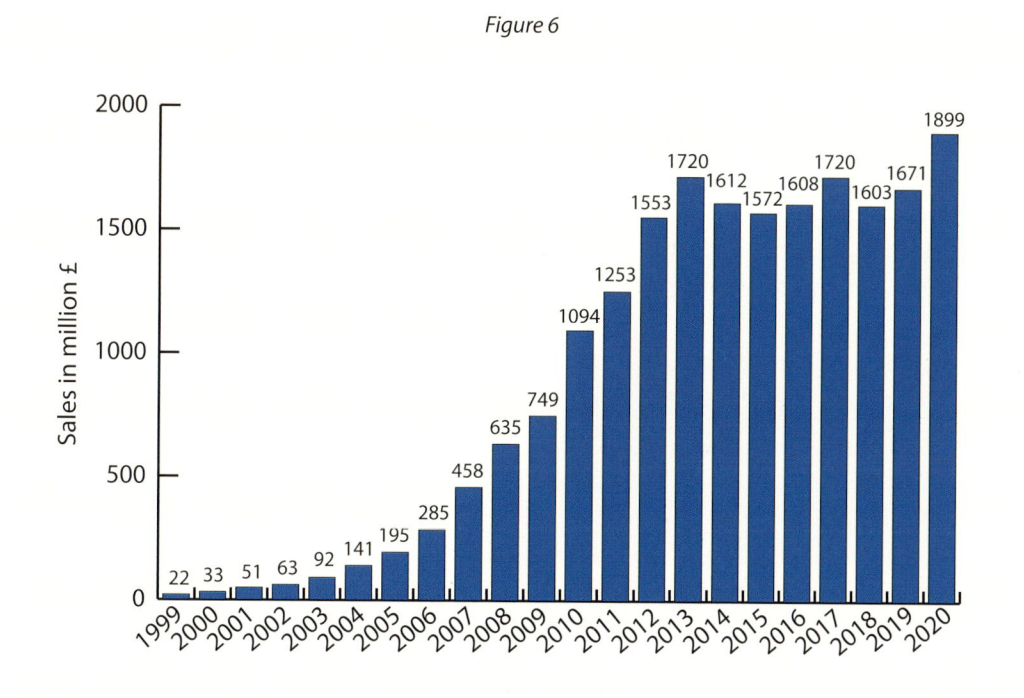

Figure 6

[Bar chart showing Sales in million £ from 1999 to 2020: 1999: 22, 2000: 33, 2001: 51, 2002: 63, 2003: 92, 2004: 141, 2005: 195, 2006: 285, 2007: 458, 2008: 635, 2009: 749, 2010: 1094, 2011: 1253, 2012: 1553, 2013: 1720, 2014: 1612, 2015: 1572, 2016: 1608, 2017: 1720, 2018: 1603, 2019: 1671, 2020: 1899]

Source: Data from 'Sales revenue of Fairtrade food and drink products in the United Kingdom from 1999 to 2020', published by Nils-Gerrit Wunsch, www.statista.com

(a) Identify the year when Fairtrade food and drink sales were at their peak. [1]

2020

1/1 mark awarded
There is one mark for identifying 2020 as the correct year.

79

PRACTICE QUESTIONS

(b) State the meaning of the term **fair trade**. [2]

> This is where the LEDC receives a salary of at least minimum wage from the MEDC that it trades with. This means the LEDC producer receives a sustainable salary where the size of the farm land does not matter and minimum wage is higher than the local wage.

1/2 marks awarded
1 mark awarded
For a basic definition.

2 marks awarded
For a more detailed definition. For example, fair trade is a strategy used to improve trading conditions in LEDCs and help farmers get paid a fair price for their products. It cuts out the middle men in the trading system, meaning more money goes to the producer and allows them to use extra income to protect the environment.

In this answer, the student mixed up the terminology in relation to minimum wage and has not addressed the issue of fair trade in enough depth.

(c) Describe **two** advantages that fair trade can bring to LEDCs. You should refer to places in your answer. [5]

> Fair trade is a sustainable solution as it allows the people in LEDCs such as Kenya to receive a fair salary. This provides the farmers with a sustainable income and the farmer and the local community can come together to co-operate and develop a reasonable payment level. This also improves relations and breaks down trade barriers, allowing the LEDC to economically develop and receive a fair amount of money for their primary production.

4/5 marks awarded
Level 1 = 1 mark
A basic answer that attempts to describe fair trade. The answer may lack reference to places.

Level 2 = 2–3 marks
A limited answer that describes the advantages of how fair trade is helping a country to develop. One place should be referenced for a Level 2 answer.

Level 3 = 4–5 marks
A detailed answer with a solid description of two of the advantages of fair trade in LEDCs (and a reference to two places).

In this case the student has given a good description for fair trade but needs to discuss an additional place.

EXAM-STYLE QUESTIONS

12. (a) Identify **one** of the Sustainable Development Goals. [1]

> Goal 1

0/1 marks awarded
There is one mark available for the accurate identification (and title) of one of the Sustainable Development Goals. Candidates must make sure that this is written out in full.

(b) Describe how this goal (above) attempts to reduce the development gap. [3]

> Goal 1 aims to end poverty in all of it forms everywhere. This is where countries must try to establish economic growth – providing jobs and equality for the people. Over 783 million people live below the poverty line of $1.90 a day. This is much lower than it has been (from 27% in 2000 to 9% in 2017). If people are receiving more money for their work, they can then pay for food, energy and accommodation, and their standard of living will improve.

3/3 marks awarded
Award 1 mark
A basic statement that attempts to describe the development goal.

Award 2 marks
A limited answer that has a basic description of the development goal but does not fully address how this goal can help to reduce the world development gap.

Award 3 marks
A detailed answer that describes the development goal and covers all aspects of the question, with relevant facts and details to support the SDG, and a full description of how the goal will be achieved.

In this case the candidate has put together a good understanding of the goal and has made good reference to how it will reduce the development gap.

13. Describe how globalisation can both help and hinder development, with reference to your case study from a BRICS country. [6]

> Globalisation is the process where the world is becoming more interconnected and interdependent. People around the world are more connected to each other than ever before. For example, Nike is a US company that bases a lot of its factories in China. This has helped China because the outside investment from MNCs such as Nike has brought better paying jobs and better standards of employment and living to the Chinese people. This has helped improve working conditions and Chinese workers have much better rights.

81

PRACTICE QUESTIONS

4/6 marks awarded

Level 1 = 1–2 marks
A basic statement that briefly looks at globalisation and might attempt to show how this could help or hinder development.

Level 2 = 3–4 marks
A limited answer that focuses on only one aspect of the question in some detail or has not gone into enough depth across both of the aspects listed in the question.

Level 3 = 5–6 marks
A detailed answer that covers all aspects of the question, with relevant facts to support the answer. It discusses the aspects that will both help and hinder development, with some reference to case study material from a BRICS country.

In this answer the student has provided some very strong case study material and the discussion of the help is good. However, the hindrance needs more detail to get the maximum marks in Level 3.

Theme D: Managing Our Environment

14. Study **Figure 7** which shows the amount of carbon dioxide emissions per capita across the United Kingdom. Answer the questions that follow.

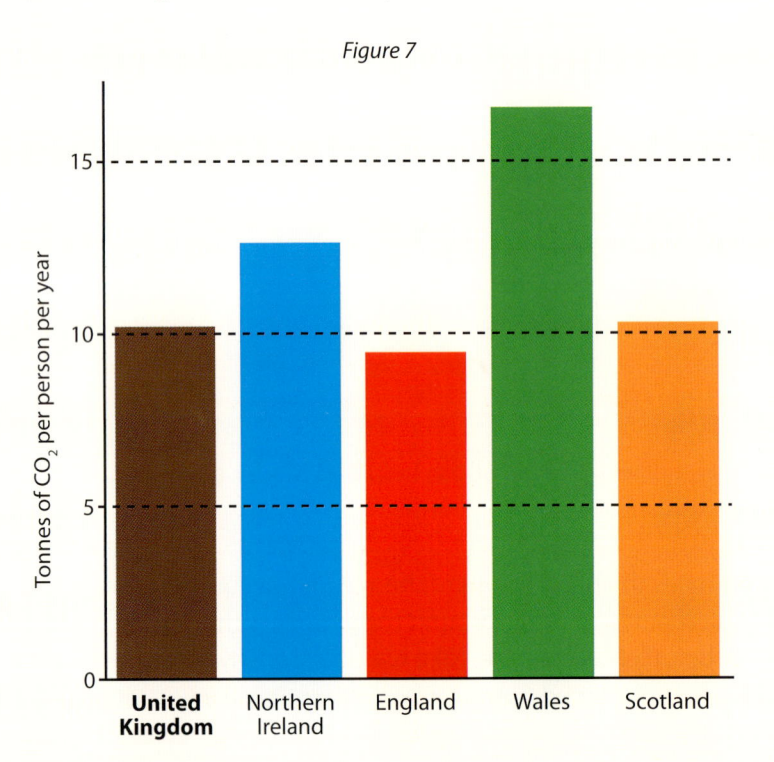

Figure 7

Source: Data from the Northern Ireland Greenhouse Gas Emissions Reduction Action Plan, February 2011

(a) Describe the pattern of carbon dioxide emissions per capita across the United Kingdom shown in **Figure 7**. [4]

EXAM-STYLE QUESTIONS

In the UK the amount of carbon dioxide emissions per person per year is just over 10 tonnes. The only area of the UK where the amount of emissions is below this is England (around 9 tonnes) but the other three regions are higher. Scotland is just over 10 tonnes and Northern Ireland and Wales are much higher than that.

3/4 marks awarded

Award 1 mark
A basic statement with no figures quoted.

Award 2–3 marks
A limited statement which refers to each of the regions on the graph and uses figures to back up the statement of description.

Award 4 marks
A detailed statement which refers to all five of the areas on the graph with figures and a statement of comparison for each.

In this case the candidate has started well, identified some of the regions and made a comparison with the UK. However, more facts and figures are needed for the final two regions (Wales and Northern Ireland).

(b) Explain how the greenhouse effect has contributed to climate change. [3]

The greenhouse effect is when thermal radiation from the surface of the Earth is bounced back to the Earth due to the build-up of greenhouse gases (such as water vapour, carbon dioxide, methane and nitrous oxide) in the atmosphere. This causes the temperature in the atmosphere to increase (global warming) which causes changes to the global climate (climate change).

3/3 marks awarded

1 mark awarded
For a basic statement.

2 marks awarded
For a limited answer in relation to the greenhouse effect and how it contributes to climate change.

3 marks awarded
For a detailed answer which includes factual information showing the link between the greenhouse effect and climate change.

In this case the student has given a clear and precise explanation of the greenhouse effect and has been able to link this as a causal factor for climate change.

15. Complete **Figure 8** below to identify the different elements of the waste hierarchy. [4]

Figure 8

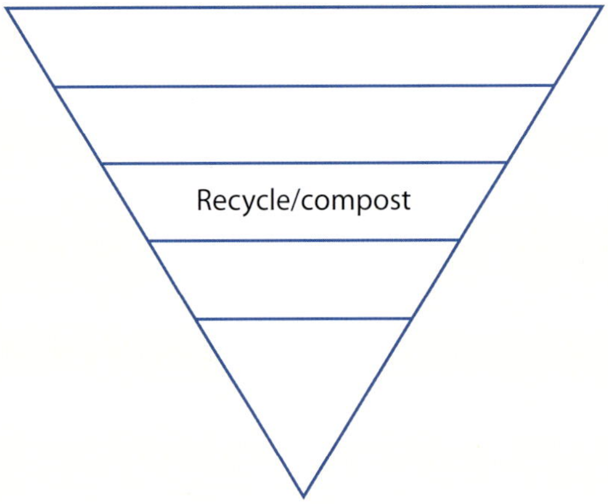
Recycle/compost

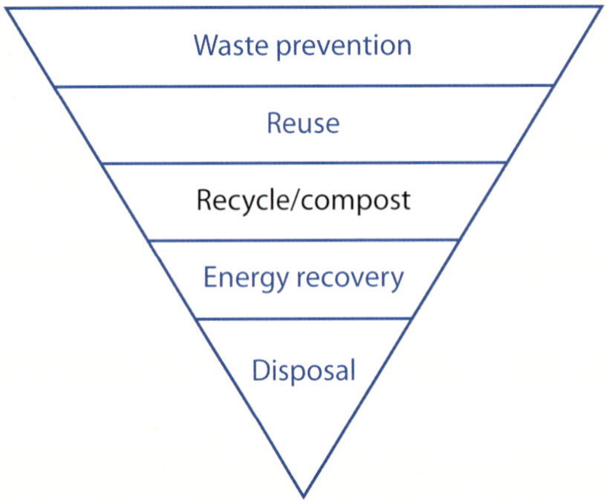
Waste prevention
Reuse
Recycle/compost
Energy recovery
Disposal

4/4 marks awarded

There is one mark for each of the correct answers on this diagram.

16. Suggest **two** ways in which the environment in tourist destinations might be negatively impacted by mass tourism. [4]

1. This could reduce the area of land available for wildlife as there is an increased desire for hotels and shopping construction to meet the tourists' needs.

2. This could increase the carbon footprint in the environment of the tourist destination as more tourists will go to that place and cause pollution.

3/4 marks awarded

Award 1 mark

For a basic statement.

Award 2 marks

For a detailed explanation of how the environment might be negatively impacted by mass tourism. This should be repeated for the second statement (2 x 2 marks).

In this case the candidate has obtained 2/2 marks for the first impact but the explanation for the second impact is not as strong and needs more development to justify full marks.

EXAM-STYLE QUESTIONS

17. State the meaning of the term **ecotourism**. [2]

> Ecotourism is when people travel to a country without causing damage to the environment as they do so and measures are put into place to protect the environment, wildlife and resources.

2/2 marks awarded

1 mark awarded
For a basic definition.

2 marks awarded
For a more detailed definition.

The candidate has put together a comprehensive description of what ecotourism is. They have clearly explained the different aspects of ecotourism so full marks can be awarded.

18. Evaluate the impacts of mass tourism on the culture and economy of tourist destinations. You should refer to named places in your answer. [8]

> The culture and economy are greatly impacted by tourism in tourist destinations such as Kenya. This is a location that attracts high levels of tourism. This can affect the economy positively. In 2010, 190,000 jobs were created by tourism which helped the local economy and made $887 million that year. However, 30% of these jobs were seasonal, so can be unreliable and do not provide income all year. Also, most of the money made from the tourists goes back to the international company and is not invested in the local community. Sometimes there are attacks on the tourists as their rich belongings might encourage robberies and kidnaps. Also, sometimes displaying the culture makes people feel like performers rather than sharing an important lesson from history.

6/8 marks awarded

Level 1 = 1–2 marks
The answer will contain some basic relevant information but might miss out on either positives or negatives or only discuss one impact.

Level 2 = 3–5 marks
A limited answer that will outline both cultural and economic impacts with some evaluation of positive or negative impacts.

Level 3 = 6–8 marks
A detailed answer that will make specific reference to at least one place and has developed both positives and negatives for both the economic and the cultural impacts. There is a fair amount of detail in the answer and the candidate is in command of the question.

In this case, the student has shown a good level of knowledge in relation to Kenya. However, the answer could have been a little more specific, especially in relation to the discussion of cultural impacts. A little deeper evaluation required here to achieve a higher Level 3 mark.

PRACTICE QUESTIONS

Revision advice

The secret ingredient to successful revision is that you must LEARN your topics. Revision can be boring and it can be difficult to stay focused. However, you have to train your brain to learn things in the depth that you need. Here are some useful tips that can help you:

1. Start your revision early and plan it carefully so that you have enough time to cover the whole subject at least three times before the exam season starts.

2. Revision is not just reading; it involves taking notes and processing information.

3. You can't do that much revision sitting at your computer. Technology provides lots of amazing new ways to support your revision but try not to become distracted by the games, the drawings and the timetables. You may need to turn off your computer, tablet or phone, or leave your devices in another room to avoid distraction.

4. Some people like to revise in short bursts (e.g. 50 minutes), with mini breaks (e.g. 10 minutes) in between to have a cup of coffee, check their phone or go for a walk. Others like to revise for longer periods and set themselves a target (e.g. 3 hours), which they aim to meet, followed by a reward such as watching a TV programme. It doesn't matter how you organise yourself – all that matters is that you put the time and effort in.

5. Remember, just because you are sitting at the desk in your bedroom doesn't mean that you are actually achieving anything. Don't fool yourself; if you don't get the work done, you won't get the marks you want. If you are struggling to focus, ask your friends and parents to check on you more often to help keep you on task.

Understanding the way that YOU learn is very important. It is unlikely that you will be able to learn and remember things in the same way that your friends do. How much revision you need to do is a very individual thing.

Revision and learning techniques

There are many different revision and learning techniques. Everyone is different, so it can be useful to practise a variety of techniques until you find the one that works best for you.

1. Condense 3

This is a traditional technique that works well if you find it difficult to remember things over a long period of time. The aim is to create a set of 'trigger' words that will help to prompt knowledge in the middle of the exam.

Step 1: Go through a particular topic and make notes about what you need to remember.

Step 2: Now go through the notes you have made and try to condense them again onto an A5 page (one side).

REVISION ADVICE

Step 3: Condense the information for a third time by taking note of the key words on your A5 page and writing them on one A3 page. Your aim is to have one big page for each major topic, packed with the key 'trigger' words that you need to remember.

Step 4: Sit and learn the trigger words. Take each word in turn and say it aloud. Put your finger on the word on the page and think about what other information this trigger word leads you to.

2. Mind maps

This technique allows you to see the 'big picture' and is great for organising information. It can also be useful when trying to work out how to answer a question. Using the example below as a template, try to draw your own mind map for each topic and use them to answer practice questions.

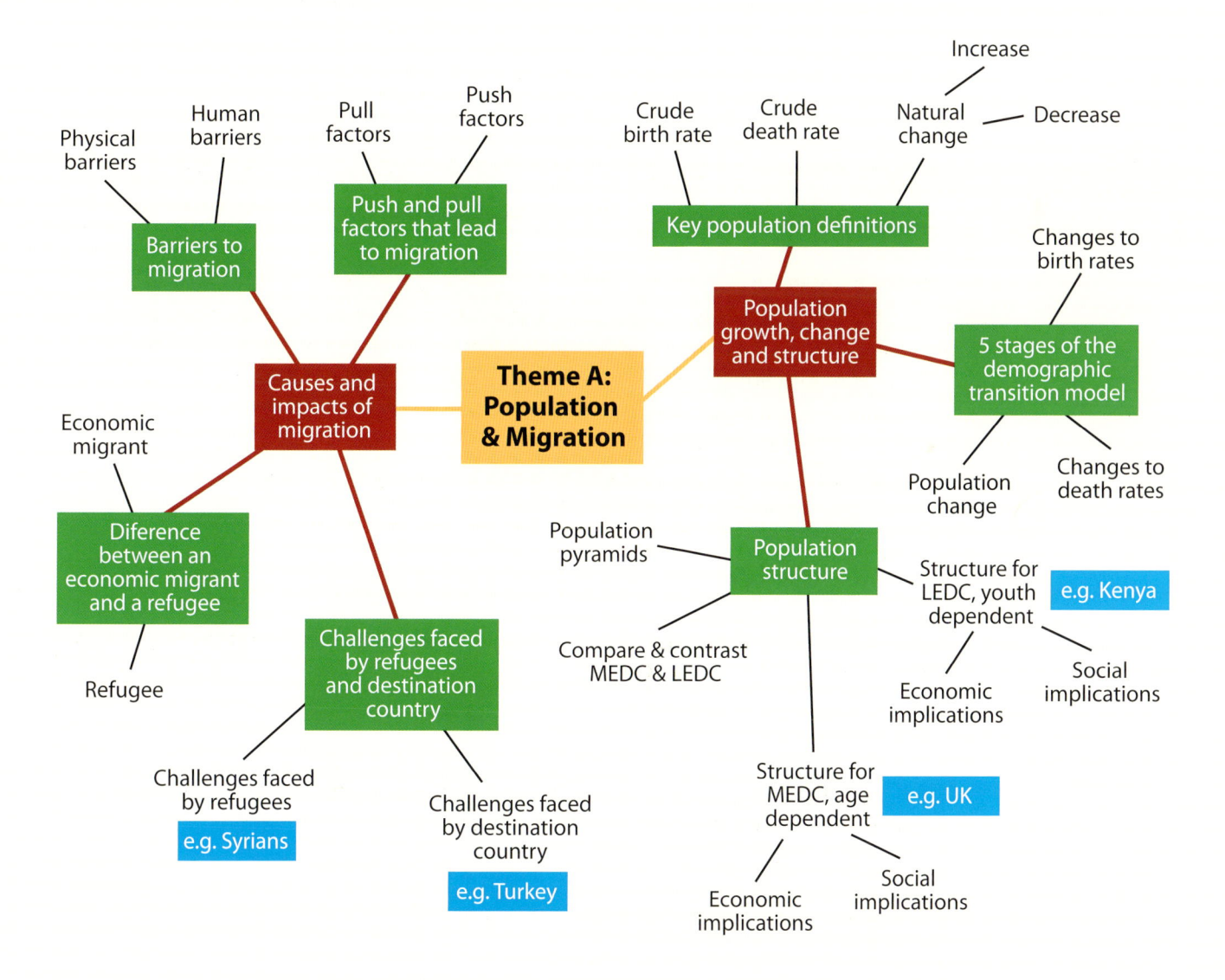

Theme A: Population & Migration

Causes and impacts of migration
- Barriers to migration
  - Physical barriers
  - Human barriers
- Push and pull factors that lead to migration
  - Pull factors
  - Push factors
- Difference between an economic migrant and a refugee
  - Economic migrant
  - Refugee
- Challenges faced by refugees and destination country
  - Challenges faced by refugees (e.g. Syrians)
  - Challenges faced by destination country (e.g. Turkey)

Population growth, change and structure
- Key population definitions
  - Crude birth rate
  - Crude death rate
  - Natural change (Increase / Decrease)
- 5 stages of the demographic transition model
  - Changes to birth rates
  - Population change
  - Changes to death rates
- Population structure
  - Population pyramids
  - Compare & contrast MEDC & LEDC
  - Structure for LEDC, youth dependent (e.g. Kenya)
    - Economic implications
    - Social implications
  - Structure for MEDC, age dependent (e.g. UK)
    - Economic implications
    - Social implications

87

3. Traffic lighting

This technique offers a simple way for you to identify:

- what you already know
- what you nearly know
- what you do not know

You can use highlighters or coloured dots as you go through your notebook to indicate how well you know and understand various parts of the course.

4. Revision cards

You might find it useful to make your own revision cards to memorise. Here are two ways to organise them:

- Make one card for each topic or case study. Pack the card with information and key facts that will help support an answer. You could even have advantages on one side and disadvantages on the other.
- You could create your own Geography 'Top Trumps' type game, where you have key facts and features on a card and you have to remember where the case study place is.

5. Make your own podcast

Although there are some very good podcasts available that may help your revision, if you make your own, you can tailor it to your own needs. There is a lot of free software online that allows you to record your own MP3, so you can sit on the bus or go to bed listening to the facts and figures from your Geography course.

Some final advice about revising Geography...

Practise your case studies

Case studies are an important part of your GCSE Geography course. You will read a lot of background information that you won't be asked about in an examination but is needed for the case study to make sense. Make sure that you learn **only what you need to know** for each case study. Learn the location, the key facts and the main points that are raised about what the case study shows.

Practise questions involving case studies as much as you can. They make up a sizeable amount of the questions in your examination paper.

Glossary

Theme A: Population and Migration

Aged dependency: A population structure where most of the people in the population are to be found above the age of 65.

Crude birth rate: The number of live births each year per thousand of the population in an area. Also known as the birth rate.

Crude death rate: The number of deaths each year per thousand of the population in an area. Also known as the death rate.

Demographic transition model: This model demonstrates how population changes over time. It shows how birth rate and death rate have influenced the total population of a place.

Dependency: The balance between the working population (aged 16–64) and the non-working population.

Destination country: The country that a migrant is trying to reach in order to improve their economic prospects or personal safety.

Economic migrant: When a migrant chooses to move in order to improve their standard of living, wage or job prospects.

Emigration: When people leave or exit a country. For example, when migrants leave Ukraine to move to Poland.

Immigration: When people move into a country. For example, migrants moving from Northern Ireland into Canada.

Migration: The permanent or semi-permanent movement of people from one place to another. Migration can take place over short or long distances and is usually a one-way movement.

Natural change: This change occurs when there is an imbalance between the birth and death rates.

GLOSSARY

Natural decrease: This happens when there is a lower birth rate than death rate, causing a decline in the number of people in an area.

Natural increase: This happens when there is a higher birth rate than death rate, causing a growth in the number of people in an area.

Population change: The population of an area can change naturally due to births and deaths, or by migration.

Population pyramid: A graph showing the specific age and sex breakdown of a population.

Population structure: The breakdown of the population by age and sex in an area. It is usually presented as a population pyramid. Most geographers will refer to the young people (under 16), the aged people (above 65) and the working population (between 16–65).

Pull factors: When a migrant voluntarily chooses to leave an area. The person is attracted to another area, usually looking for a better life, better standard of living or more personal freedom.

Push factors: When a migrant is forced to leave an area. The person is motivated to move out of an area due to reasons such as war or famine.

Refugee: A person who is fleeing from events such as civil wars or natural disasters but not necessarily facing persecution.

Youth dependency: A population structure where most of the people in the population are to be found under the age of 15.

Theme B: Changing Urban Areas

Central business district (CBD): The core area of the city's business life where businesses, offices and retail are located.

Gentrification: When richer people move into an urban area and replace the poorer people who used to live there. This changes the character of the area.

Inner city: The area of a city that usually surrounds the CBD. This area used to be the main source of income for the city. Here heavy industrial factories and low-cost residential areas were often built very close to each other.

Land-use zones: A series of areas or zones within a city (CBD, inner city, suburbs and rural fringe). Land in each zone shares the same function or aspect of city life.

Rural-urban fringe: The area of the city developed from the 1960s at the edge of the suburbs. Sometimes it can be difficult to see where the city ends and the countryside begins, as there is a mix of rural and urban land use.

Settlement: A place where people live and work. It can be as large as a megacity such as London or as small as dispersed, individual houses found in farming areas such as the Lake District.

Settlement function: The main economic and social activity or role of a place.

Shanty town: A spontaneous settlement built within a city. Also known as a favela. This area often features unplanned, poor-quality housing and lacks basic amenities, such as clean water.

Suburbs: The areas of a city that sit beyond the inner city. These areas of large-scale suburban residential development grew in the UK throughout the twentieth century. People chose to move to this space on the edge of the city to have access to larger, better-quality homes.

Urban planning scheme: A plan put into place (usually by the local government) to change and improve the urban environment.

Urban regeneration: When an urban area is upgraded. The aim is to improve both the economic and social spaces within a city.

GLOSSARY

Theme C: Contrasts in World Development

Appropriate technology: Technology suited to the needs, skills, knowledge, resources and wealth of local people.

BRICS: The countries of Brazil, Russia, India, China and South Africa. These are the five main emerging markets or economies across the world.

Development: The quality of life of humans within a country or area. It is linked to the wealth and progress of the area.

Development gap: The difference in economic activity, wealth and social measures between the rich MEDCs and poorer LEDCs.

Economic indicators: A set of factors used to assess the amount of money or wealth within a country and how the people actually earn that wealth (e.g. GNP or GNI).

Fair trade: A strategy used to provide an organised approach to help producers in LEDCs gain better trading conditions.

Globalisation: The process of the world becoming more interconnected and interdependent. People around the world are more connected to each other than ever before as jobs and industry spread across our world.

Human Development Index (HDI): A measure of development, used by the United Nations, which combines indicators of life expectancy, educational attainment and income into a composite measure (of both social and economic indicators).

LEDC (Less Economically Developed Country): Usually a poorer country found in South America, Africa or Asia.

MEDC (More Economically Developed Country): Usually a rich country found in Western Europe or North America.

Primary activities: Jobs or economic activities where people are involved in collecting and working with raw materials or resources, such as farming, mining, quarrying and fishing.

Social indicators: A set of factors used to assess how well a country is developing in the key areas that affect people, such as health, education and diet.

Sustainable Development Goals (SDGs): A set of targets, agreed by the United Nations, aimed at ending poverty around the world, helping protect the planet and ensuring a new prosperity for everyone. The 17 SDGs (or the 'Global Goals') included over 169 separate targets.

Theme D: Managing Our Environment

Biofuels: Also known as biogas or biomass. A renewable energy source that uses fermented animal or plant waste to create power. Power is generated as the biological material rots and creates chemical energy.

Carbon footprint: The total set of greenhouse gas emissions that are caused by an organisation, event, product or person. Often this is taken as a measure of carbon dioxide emissions.

Climate change: The long-term, global change in temperature and precipitation patterns. Many scientists believe this change has been accelerated by human activity, including the greenhouse effect.

Ecotourism: A sustainable type of tourism, which protects the wildlife and natural resources of the host area.

Greenhouse effect: The process where thermal radiation from the surface of the Earth is bounced back to the Earth due to the build-up of greenhouse gases (such as carbon dioxide and methane) in the atmosphere causing temperatures to increase.

Mass tourism: When large numbers of people go on holiday to the same resort, usually at the same time of year, often as part of a package deal.

Renewable energy source: A sustainable source of energy production (e.g. solar, wind or biofuels). The energy can be naturally replaced and used repeatedly.

Responsible tourism: Any form of tourism where visitors do their best to minimise any negative social, environmental or economic impacts on the local people.

Solar energy: A renewable energy source that uses the sun to generate power. The sun's light and heat is converted into electricity and used to heat water.

Sustainable tourism: Tourism that takes full account of its current and future economic, social and environmental impacts. It addresses the needs of visitors, the industry, the environment and host communities.

Waste hierarchy: A method used to rank waste management options in order of sustainability. Top priority goes to measures that prevent waste in the first place, followed by preparing waste for reuse, then recycling, then recovery and finally disposal.

Wind energy: A renewable energy source that uses the force of the wind to turn the sails on a turbine and generate power.

Copyright

All rights reserved. No part of this publication may be reproduced, stored in a retrieval system or transmitted in any form or by any means, electronic, mechanical, photocopying, scanning, recording or otherwise, without the prior written permission of the copyright owners and publisher of this book.

Copyright has been acknowledged to the best of our ability. If there are any inadvertent errors or omissions, we shall be happy to correct them in any future editions.

Credits

Where information or data has been used, sources are cited within the body of the book.

The following photographs are included with the kind permission of the copyright holders. The numbers denote page numbers:

Benny Zheng: 60

Colin Williams Photography: 22, 29, 76

COP21 / Alamy Stock Photo: 59

David Dixon: 58

Fancisco Antunes: 32

Hippo Roller: 45, 46

iStock: 52, 62, 88

Mara Intrepids Camp: 64

Tim Manson: 23, 74

Licences

The data in the tables on page 35 is licensed under the Creative Commons Attribution 4.0 International license (CC-BY 4.0) license.

The diagram on page 36 and data in the table on page 37 is licensed under the Creative Commons Attribution 3.0 IGO (CC BY 3.0 IGO) license.

The images on pages 32 and 58 are licensed under the Creative Commons Share-alike 2.0 Generic license.

The diagrams on pages 8 and 25 are Crown Copyright and reproduced under the terms of the Open Government Licence v.3.

The map on page 73 is Crown Copyright and is reproduced with the permission of Land & Property Services under delegated authority from the Controller of Her Majesty's Stationery Office, Crown copyright and database right 2023 PMLPA No 100496

'Basic map skills' on page 20 was adapted from © CCEA 2023: Reproduced with permission of the Northern Ireland Council for the Curriculum, Examinations and Assessment.

'Water features' and 'Tourist information' on page 21 is based upon Crown Copyright and is reproduced with the permission of Land & Property Services under delegated authority from the Controller of Her Majesty's Stationery Office, Crown copyright and database right 2023 PMLPA No 100496